EXPLORING CAREERS IN SCIENCE

EXPLORING CAREERS IN SCIENCE

By

Stanley Jay Shapiro

RICHARDS ROSEN PRESS, INC.
New York, N.Y. 10010

Published in 1981 by Richards Rosen Press, Inc.
29 East 21st Street, New York, N.Y. 10010

First Edition

Library of Congress Cataloging in Publication Data

Shapiro, Stanley Jay.
    Exploring careers in science.

    (Careers in depth)
    SUMMARY: Discusses careers in the physical, life,
environmental, conservation, and mathematical sciences
and how to prepare for them.
    1. Science—Vocational guidance. [1. Science—
Vocational guidance. 2. Vocational guidance] I. Title.
Q147.S48   502.3   80–28889
ISBN 0–8239–0535–7

Manufactured in the United States of America

To Sabar, the magician,
and Princess Barbara

About the Author

Stanley Shapiro is a teacher of chemistry at James Madison High School in Brooklyn, New York. He specializes in working with gifted teenagers who want to pursue professional careers in science, mathematics, and medicine.

Dr. Shapiro grew up in Washington, D.C., where, through the public school science fair program, he developed an interest in science. As a high school student, he won more than twenty local and national awards, including three National First Place Awards in the Future Scientists of America Science Fair, the Academy of Science Medal, the Dow Chemical Award, the Smithsonian Award, and the Honor's Group Award of the Westinghouse Science Talent Search.

He received a bachelor of science degree in chemistry from the American University in Washington, D.C., and a master's degree in organic chemistry from New York University. Dr. Shapiro received a doctorate in science education from New York University in 1978. His research study was *A Multimedia Project for the Independent Instruction of Allied Health Students in the Application of Mathematical Skills to Science Problems in their Curricula.*

From 1974 to 1977 he was the science curriculum specialist for the Division of Allied Health at New York City Community College, City University of New York. At the college, he worked on the development of a multimedia learning center, where students could use television, audiotapes, slides, filmstrips, workbooks, and laboratory facilities to learn science skills. Prior to that he was a biochemist for the Gillette Research Institute, an assistant conservator for the Smithsonian Institution, and a science writer for the NBC-TV show *It's Academic.*

Dr. Shapiro is a member of the American Association for the Advancement of Science, the National Science Teachers Association, Phi Delta Kappa, the American Chemical Society, the Chemistry Teachers Club, the New York Zoological Society, and the Science Council of New York City. He is a consultant to the National Science Foundation on teacher development projects in science.

He lives in New York City with his wife, Marjorie, his eleven-year-old daughter, Rachel, and two cats, Pussy Wussy and Kitty Witty. He enjoys golf, tennis, swimming, theater, ballet, and chamber music.

Acknowledgments

The information gathered for this book came from many sources. Of particular usefulness were the *Occupational Outlook Handbook,* prepared by the Bureau of Labor Statistics; the *Selected Characteristics of Persons in Fields of Science and Engineering:* 1976, prepared by the Bureau of the Census; Mel Guttman's *Comprehensive Guide to College and Career Planning,* published by Richards Rosen Press; Walter S. Smith and Kala M. Stroup's *Science Career Exploration for Women,* published by the National Science Teachers Association; and three volumes from the Scientific Manpower Commission: *Supply and Demand for Scientists and Engineers* by Betty M. Vetter, *Science and Engineering Careers: A Bibliography* prepared by Eleanor Babco, and *Salaries of Scientists, Engineers and Technicians* prepared by Eleanor Babco.

Many professional organizations and societies offered a great deal of help. I wish to thank the American Association for the Advancement of Science, the American Astronomical Society, the American Chemical Society, the American Federation of Information Processing Societies, the American Forestry Association, the American Geologic Institute, the American Geophysical Institute, the American Institute of Biological Sciences, the American Institute of Physics, the American Meteorological Society, the American Physiological Society, the American Society of Agronomy, the Institute of Food Technology, the International Oceanographic Foundation, the Manufacturing Chemists Association, the Mathematical Association of America, the National Science Teachers Association, and the Society of Exploration Geophysicists.

Several United States government agencies and departments supplied valuable information. These include the Bureau of Labor Statistics, the Bureau of the Census, the National Science Foundation, the Department of Agriculture, the National Oceanic and Atmospheric Administration, the Department of the Interior, the National Aeronautics and Space Administration, and the Civil Service Commission.

I would also like to thank the following private corporations for their help and assistance: Bell Laboratories, Dupont, General Electric, International Business Machines, and Mobil Oil Company.

Preface

Many people become interested in science because of courses in school or from experiences in their lives. They like to take radios apart to find out how they work. They pick up seashells along the beach and wonder what kinds of creatures once inhabited them. They see science adventure films and are excited by the marvels of technology. They enjoy watching their science teacher produce a violent explosion from an invisible gas. Some people are not curious about how a bird can fly or why a volcano erupts, but people who like science are interested in learning all they can about nature.

Science is for people who love to solve fascinating problems. Science holds the hope that there is an order to the universe, which, with careful study, can be understood and used to benefit all mankind. For many people science is a wonderful career. They are happy to be paid for spending their days investigating the secrets of the universe.

I guess you like science, too. However, you are probably not very sure about what scientists and mathematicians really do, where they work, how much they are paid, how much schooling they need, or, probably, what area of science is best for you. Well, that is just what this book is going to help you find out. We will first explain what the scientific enterprise is all about, and then we will discuss the main branches of science. Once you have narrowed down the fields in which you are most interested, we can explore the opportunities and requirements of the various occupations in detail.

If you have any questions as you read this book, see your guidance counselor or your science teacher. They will be glad to help you choose a career that is suited to your interests and capabilities and that will be exciting and rewarding to you.

Contents

EXPLORING CAREERS IN SCIENCE

Chapter **I**

What Is Science?

So you think you would like to be a scientist or a mathematician. That's great! This country can use lots of bright, hard-working people in its scientific and technical workforce. In 1979 about one and one-half million people, nearly one-eighth of all professional workers, were working in science. In that year over five billion dollars was spent for research and development in science. In the next ten years there will be over 150,000 openings for scientists and mathematicians. Perhaps you will be one of the new workers in America's most vital enterprise.

Science is the principal reason for our nation's growth and the high standard of living enjoyed by most Americans. Science allows us to communicate with the world by telephone, radio, and television. It has revolutionized transportation. Planes fly, in three and one-half hours, distances that once took weeks to cross. Trucks, railways, supertankers, and, soon, rocketships carry manufactured goods and cargo around the world and to neighboring planets. The automobile has allowed a freedom of mobility to the average person that could not be imagined by princes a century ago.

Our everyday life is surrounded by the inventions of science. The fabrics we wear, the appliances in our homes, and the stereos, tape decks, TV's, and movies that we use for entertainment all come to us through the work of scientists and mathematicians. Through medical discoveries, science has made it possible for people to live longer, healthier lives. Agriculture, too, has benefited from science. Two hundred years ago, about 90 out of every 100 Americans lived on farms. Today, less than 5 percent of our population are farmers. As you can see, the world depends on the progress and changes brought about by science to maintain and improve our civilization.

What Is Science?

Since you may be spending your life working in science, let us carefully define it. Science is learning about nature. Scientists try to understand the living and physical world through observation, study, and experi-

3

mentation. Science is the opposite of superstition. It is a body of knowledge based not on fear and ignorance but rather on a careful, well-organized analysis of the laws of nature and the creatures and objects of the universe.

Two hundred years ago, most people thought that lightning was caused by gods or demons. They could see the lightning bolt and the terrible destruction it produced. However, instead of looking for a natural cause, they relied on superstition for its explanation. Benjamin Franklin, America's first great physicist, could not accept this nonscientific thinking. To investigate lightning, he flew a rain-soaked kite in a thunderstorm. Lightning struck the kite and the energy flowed down the wet string to a metal key, causing a discharge at the end. Franklin observed that the shock was the same as the kind he got when he walked across a rug on a dry day and touched a metal door knob—it was static electricity. If lightning, Franklin reasoned, was only a more powerful form of the electricity that he had experimented with in his laboratory, then he could control it. He constructed tall metal poles from the ground to the tops of chimneys on many of the houses and barns around colonial Philadelphia. When the next thunderstorm came, lightning hit several of the rods, but the electricity was carried to the ground, and none of the buildings was damaged. Franklin used science to save lives and property, and he showed that the devil was no excuse for ignorance.

What Is a Scientist?

A scientist is a person who has curiosity and imagination. He or she wants to know what things are and how events happen. Scientists study nature very carefully and use the facts they learn to benefit mankind.

Many people can look at a flower and see that it is beautiful. A poet or an artist may even notice qualities that make the blossom especially lovely. When a scientist looks at a flower, however, he or she not only thinks about its decorativeness, but examines the plant in order to understand the function of the pistil, the stigma, the style, the ovule, the ovary, the stamen, the anther, the petal, and the sepal. A scientist tries to discover how these parts help the plant survive? He or she asks: What purpose does the scent serve? How much sunlight and water does it need? What chemicals produce the brilliant colors? How does the pollen leave the plant? What signals the opening of the bud? Scientists want to know everything about the flower and its role in the living world.

The curiosity of scientists allows them the patience and the time to study the flower. Their imagination lets them use their knowledge of the plant in many productive ways, such as in the manufacture of dyes, perfumes, and pharmaceuticals.

The Two Realms of Science

Science may be divided into *pure science* and *applied science*. Pure science, which is sometimes called *research science*, attempts to explain the basic facts and principles of life and the laws of the universe. Applied science, sometimes called *developmental science*, uses the information discovered by the pure scientists in ways that will directly help mankind. The laser was a scientific invention developed through pure research into the nature of light energy. Its many uses, which include a microscalpel for eye surgeons, a playback "needle" for home videorecorders, an extremely accurate measuring device, a carrier for telecommunications, and a space-age weapon, were developed through the efforts of applied scientists.

In our consumer world, we are usually more familiar with the products developed by applied scientists than with the fundamental theories and facts discovered by the pure scientists and mathematicians. We know that Alexander Graham Bell invented the telephone; Thomas Alva Edison invented the phonograph, the incandescent electric light, and moving pictures; and Guglielmo Marconi sent the first radio transmission. All their inventions, however, were based on the pioneering, but lesser known, basic research of mathematicians and scientists such as James Clerk Maxwell, Jean-Baptiste-Joseph Fourier, Isaac Newton, and Pierre-Simon LaPlace. These scientists discovered the functions and properties of electromagnetic waves, which led the inventors to their inventions.

How Scientists Solve Problems

A scientist is interested mainly in events that can happen again. By repeating an experiment, a measurement, or an observation, a scientist may discover the cause of an event or a specific mathematical relationship that will help in the understanding of many similar phenomena. The scientist often changes one part of the experiment slightly, in order to investigate more precisely how nature works. So that other scientists can accept the findings, a good researcher designs his experiment so that it can be replicated by others with the same result.

Let us look at one of the first controlled scientific experiments. Three hundred years ago most people thought that flies were produced spontaneously (all by themselves, without any parents) from rotten meat because no one had ever seen a fly's egg. An Italian, Francesco Redi, believed otherwise, so he set up an experiment to find the answer. He placed pieces of meat in several bottles. Half of the bottles he sealed, and half he left open. The meat turned putrid in all of the bottles, but there were maggots (baby flies) only in the uncovered ones. He repeated the experiment, but this time, instead of sealing half the bottles, he merely covered them with a thin fabric, and as before, he left the other half open to the air. Again, only in those bottles which adult flies could enter freely were maggots found. Redi was able, by his systematic experimentation, to prove that maggots came from eggs laid on the meat by flies and were not spontaneously generated. His carefully controlled experiment, which was easily repeatable, changed the way in which many learned people looked at the world.

Scientists study a great range of facts and events. Physicists try to find new ways to make atomic energy safe and useful. Chemists try to produce new materials, such as polyester fibers and plastics, to make life easier. Medical researchers seek ways to make people healthier. Biologists study the lives of plants and animals to encourage their growth and to provide for mankind. Scientists try to discover what happens, how it happens, and why it happens. They are using tools and equipment far more complicated than Redi's bottles or Franklin's kite, yet they still must rely on planned, careful observation and open-minded curiosity. If you wonder about nature and have a great deal of patience and "stick-to-itiveness" you might do very well in a scientific career. This book will show you what opportunities there are for you in science.

Chapter II

Occupations in Science and Mathematics

Jobs in the sciences can usually be divided into four broad categories: (1) physical sciences; (2) life sciences; (3) environmental sciences; and (4) mathematics. Let us look briefly into these four areas.

The Physical Sciences

The largest group of scientists study the physical world. Some 40,000 new physical scientists will be hired in the next five years. Most physical scientists are chemists. Chemists are interested in taking substances apart and rearranging them in new ways. Most chemists work in private industry. They help develop better textiles, paper, rubber, plastics, drugs, metals, fuels, and other products.

Physics is the other major branch of the physical sciences. Physics is concerned with matter and energy. Physicists study mechanics, heat, light, sound, electricity, magnetism, and the properties of matter. The two newest occupations in physics deal with nuclear energy and the principles of sending spacecraft on missions throughout the solar system. Most physicists work in colleges and universities, where they teach and do research. In private industry, physicists work for companies that develop aerospace, electronic, or defense-related products.

The Life Sciences

Life scientists study living things, from the smallest microbe to the largest whale. The majority of life scientists teach or do research in colleges and universities. Over 60,000 new jobs will be available in the life sciences during the next five years.

Biological scientists are the largest group of life scientists. Biologists are concerned with collecting, naming, classifying, examining, and describing living things. There are many occupations within the field of biology. For example, biologists who study plants are called botanists, those who study animals are called zoologists, and those interested in

7

prehistoric life are called paleontologists. Biologists are not merely concerned with a description of life forms; they are also interested in learning how and why organisms act as they do.

The other large group of life scientists are the medical scientists. They study how the body works and try to discover ways to keep it functioning in good health. Medical science is the fastest growing group within the life sciences. Physicians, nurses, dentists, veterinarians, and so on are generally not considered medical scientists. They are concerned, basically, with the delivery of health care, instead of the scientific research aspect. Medical scientists discover the principles and develop the tools and techniques with which the medical practitioners help their patients.

Environmental Scientists

Environmental scientists study the earth, its oceans, and its atmosphere. They are concerned with understanding our planet, in controlling pollution, in weather prediction, and in developing natural resources. There will be approximately 35,000 new jobs for environmental scientists in the next five years.

The largest group of environmental scientists are the geologists. Geologists study the earth. They learn how mountains rise up and are worn down, how rivers and glaciers flow, and they study the action of volcanoes and earthquakes. Energy companies hire most geologists to help find coal, petroleum, and other minerals beneath the surface of the earth.

Meteorologists are environmental scientists who study the weather and the atmosphere. Most meteorologists work for the National Weather Service or for the armed forces. Their chief concern is predicting the weather. Some meteorologists are involved in basic research into the causes of weather, with the goal of eventually controlling rain, hurricanes, and tornados.

Oceanographers study the sea. The oceans cover more than 70 percent of the earth and affect all life. Oceanographers work with meteorologists to study the ways the ocean and the atmosphere act upon each other to create weather. Oceanographers investigate the composition of seawater, the structure of the ocean floor, the currents, the tides, and the waves. Many are exploring ways to harvest the animal and plant life in the seas to increase our food supply.

Conservation scientists are environmental scientists who protect, develop, and manage our natural resources such as forests, rangelands, wildlife, soil, air, and water. Most conservationists work for the federal or state governments, where they offer lumber companies, land developers, farmers, and industrialists assistance and advice on how to conserve and protect resources.

Mathematics

The English scientist Roger Bacon in 1267 wrote, "Mathematics is the gate and key of the sciences." Science uses mathematics for exact descriptions and for formulas that describe the laws and relationships in nature. Many scientific problems have become so complicated that only highly trained mathematicians can attempt to find the answers. There should be approximately 5,000 openings for classical mathematicians in the next five years.

Mathematicians analyze and interpret the data that scientists have discovered from their observations and experiments. If a new drug is discovered, it cannot be sold until hundreds of tests have been statistically analyzed proving it safe and effective. The trajectory of rockets and missiles and the guidance systems for aircraft, ships, and submarines are carefully computed by mathematicians.

Mathematicians also lay the theoretical groundwork for new advances in science that may not be achieved for decades to come but may someday revolutionize the way we live. In 1854 Bernard Riemann, for instance, invented a seemingly impractical form of geometry that was not used for half a century until Albert Einstein relied on it as the basis for the theory of relativity. Einstein's theory, too, had to wait nearly thirty years before it was incorporated by physicists in the creation of atomic power.

Within the last two decades, a new field has developed for people with a keen ability in mathematics. It is the computer industry. There will be over 9,000 openings a year for computer mathematicians. These jobs are not for computer operators nor for sales representatives who market computer services and hardware. They are for highly trained persons who can devise plans for solving specific problems with the computer. Computer scientists develop ways in which the computer can help business and scientific research. They help engineers build bridges and medical researchers test the effectiveness of a drug. They develop mathematical models for designing aerodynamically sound vehicles, they work on guidance systems for aircraft and ships, and they help grocery stores with their inventories. Computer mathematics is a growing field that will offer many opportunities in the future.

General Job Outlook for Scientists and Mathematicians

Each year there should be over 30,000 job openings for mathematicians and scientists in the United States. Opportunities are expected to expand well into the twenty-first century. The energy problem, the increasing awareness of health needs, the commercial development of outer space, the computer boom, the surge in electronics, and the growth of telecommunications all point to an enlarging need for scientifically trained persons.

More scientists will be needed to develop new technologies and better products. In addition, many technically trained specialists will be required to solve the problems of air, water, and noise pollution. Research and development will continue to increase throughout the next decade in both industry and government, requiring the skills and minds of people who love science.

In 1979 the U.S. Department of Labor published its predictions for job openings in the scientific and mathematical occupations. The report was written before the energy crisis began in the summer of 1979, and before nuclear construction projects were temporarily halted following the accident at Three Mile Island. However, it is a good basis for planning your future. The following is a summary of the report with some observations. The base year for this survey was 1976. The average salary for male professional workers in 1976 was $16,000. The average salary for female workers in 1976 was $11,000.

Conservation Scientists
  Foresters:
    Degree Requirements: A bachelor's degree with a major in forestry; however, because of the scarcity of jobs in the field, most employers require applicants with advanced degrees. Teaching and research require a Ph.D. degree.
    Average Salary in 1976: $18,000
    Average Federal Salary in 1978: $24,000
    Employment in 1976: 25,000
    Jobs Available Each Year (1976–85): 1,100
    Graduates Each Year (predicted):
      Bachelor's Degrees 2,700
      Master's Degrees 500
      Doctor's Degrees 150
  Range Managers:
    Degree Requirements: A bachelor's degree with a major in range management, range science, or a closely related field. Research and teaching require an advanced degree.
    Average Salary in 1976: $18,000
    Average Federal Salary in 1978: $19,000
    Employment in 1976: 3,000
    Jobs Available Each Year (1976–85): 200
    Graduates Each Year (predicted):
      Bachelor's Degrees 175
      Master's Degrees 40
      Doctor's Degrees 20
  Soil Conservationists:
    Degree Requirements: A degree in agronomy or a closely related field, such as agricultural education or wildlife biology. Research and teaching require an advanced degree.
    Average Salary in 1976: $18,000
    Average Federal Salary in 1978: $22,000

Employment in 1976: 7,500
Jobs Available Each Year (1976–85): 400
Graduates Each Year (predicted):
     Bachelor's Degrees 1,000
     Master's Degrees 300
     Doctor's Degrees 175

Environmental Scientists
 Geologists:
    Degree Requirements: A bachelor's degree with a major in earth science
    or geology is appropriate training for many entry jobs; however, an
    advanced degree is necessary for promotion. Most research and teach-
    ing positions require a Ph.D.
    Average Salary in 1976: $24,000
    Average Federal Salary in 1978: $27,500
    Employment in 1976: 34,000
    Jobs Available Each Year (1976–85): 2,300 (probably closer to 3,000
    due to the energy crisis)
    Graduates Each Year (predicted):
       Bachelor's Degrees 5,000
       Master's Degrees 1,250
       Doctor's Degrees 375
 Geophysicists:
    Degree Requirements: A bachelor's degree in geophysics or a related
    field is appropriate for many entry jobs; however, an advanced degree
    is necessary for promotion. Most research and teaching positions re-
    quire an advanced degree.
    Average Salary in 1976: $24,500
    Average Federal Salary in 1978: $28,500
    Employment in 1976: 12,000
    Jobs Available Each Year (1976–85): 800 (probably closer to 1,000 due
    to the energy crisis)
    Graduates Each Year (predicted):
       Bachelor's Degrees 100
       Master's Degrees 60
       Doctor's Degrees 30
 Meteorologists:
    Degree Requirements: A bachelor's degree in meteorology is the mini-
    mum requirement; however, many employers insist on an advanced
    degree. Most research and teaching positions require an advanced
    degree.
    Average Salary in 1976: $25,000
    Average Federal Salary in 1978: $28,500
    Employment in 1976: 5,500
    Jobs Available Each Year (1976–85): 200
    Graduates Each Year (predicted):
       Bachelor's Degrees 375
       Master's Degrees 200
       Doctor's Degrees 60

Oceanographers:
Degree Requirements: A Ph.D. in oceanography, the natural sciences, or engineering is required for a job as an oceanographer. A bachelor's degree is sufficient for beginning jobs as laboratory or research assistants.
Average Salary in 1976: $23,000
Average Federal Salary in 1978: $26,000
Employment in 1976: 2,700
Jobs Available Each Year (1976–85): 150
Graduates Each Year (predicted):

Bachelor's Degrees..................... 250
Master's Degrees 150
Doctor's Degrees 80

Life Scientists
Biochemists:
Degree Requirements: A Ph.D. degree usually is necessary for biochemical research and for advancement to management and administrative jobs. A bachelor's degree may be sufficient for entry-level jobs as research technicians and assistants.
Average Salary in 1976: $24,000
Average Federal Salary in 1978: $26,000
Employment in 1976: 12,700
Jobs Available Each Year (1976–85): 600
Graduates Each Year (predicted):

Bachelor's Degrees 1,600
Master's Degrees..................... 250
Doctor's Degrees..................... 430

Life Scientists:
Degree Requirements: A bachelor's degree is adequate for some technician or technologist work; however, an advanced degree is required for most jobs. A Ph.D. is the usual requirement for teaching and research positions. Medical research may require an M.D. or D.D.S. degree.
Average Salary in 1976: $20,300
Average Federal Salary in 1978: $25,500
Employment in 1976: 205,000
Jobs Available Each Year (1976–85): 12,000
Graduates Each Year (predicted):

Bachelor's Degrees 80,000
Master's Degrees..................... 12,000
Doctor's Degrees..................... 5,500

Mathematics Occupations
Classical Mathematicians:
Degree Requirements: Employers usually require an advanced degree, although private industry hires a few persons with bachelor's degrees. A Ph.D. is required to teach in a university or college and to engage in research.

Average Salary in 1976: $23,000
Average Federal Salary in 1978: $27,000
Employment in 1976: 38,000
Jobs Available Each Year (1976–85): 1,000
Graduates Each Year (predicted):

        Bachelor's Degrees 15,000
        Master's Degrees 3,250
        Doctor's Degrees 675

Statisticians:
    Degree Requirements: A bachelor's degree in statistics or mathematics
    is adequate for many entry-level positions; however, for some jobs a
    bachelor's degree in economics or another applied field with a minor
    in statistics is preferable. An advanced degree is required for some
    positions, such as teaching. Advancement often requires advanced
    degrees.
    Average Salary in 1976: $24,000
    Average Federal Salary in 1978: $26,000
    Employment in 1976: 24,000
    Jobs Available Each Year (1976–85): 1,500
    Graduates Each Year (predicted):

        Bachelor's Degrees 250
        Master's Degrees 475
        Doctor's Degrees 150

Computer Mathematicians (Systems Analysts):
    Degree Requirements: No one way of preparing for a job in this field.
    Generally, a bachelor's degree with specialized computer training is
    the minimum educational requirement. A job in a bank may require
    an accounting or business degree, whereas a scientific organization
    may require a degree in science or engineering. A bachelor's degree
    in computer science is becoming more readily available, but should
    be backed up with a minor in an applied field. Most research and
    advanced work requires a Ph.D.
    Average Salary in 1976: $20,000
    Average Federal Salary in 1978: $25,000
    Employment in 1976: 160,000
    Jobs Available Each Year (1976–85): 7,600
    Graduates Each Year in Systems Analysis (predicted):

        Bachelor's Degrees 90
        Master's Degrees 90
        Doctor's Degrees 3

Physical Scientists
  Astronomers:
    Degree Requirements: A Ph.D. is an absolute necessity. Persons who
    have less education may qualify for some assistant-level jobs; however,
    advancement is open only to those with a doctorate.
    Average Salary in 1976: $25,100
    Average Federal Salary in 1978: $35,000
    Employment in 1976: 2,000

Jobs Available Each Year (1976–85): 40
Graduates Each Year (predicted):
      Bachelor's Degrees...................... 120
      Master's Degrees 80
      Doctor's Degrees 120

Chemists:

Degree Requirements: A bachelor's degree in chemistry is usually the minimum requirement for many jobs in analysis and testing, quality control, or as research assistants. Graduate training is necessary for senior-level work in research and development. A Ph.D. is required for college and university teaching.

Average Salary in 1976: $23,000
Average Federal Salary in 1978: $27,000
Employment in 1976: 148,000
Jobs Available Each Year (1976–85): 6,500
Graduates Each Year (predicted):
      Bachelor's Degrees 11,000
      Master's Degrees 2,000
      Doctor's Degrees 1,500

Physicists:

Degree Requirements: A master's degree in physics is usually the minimum requirement for most jobs; however, a Ph.D. is required by many companies and by all colleges. A doctorate is necessary for senior research positions and for advancement.

Average Salary in 1976: $23,000
Average Federal Salary in 1978: $31,500
Employment in 1976: 48,000
Jobs Available Each Year (1976–85): 1,100
Graduates Each Year (predicted):
      Bachelor's Degrees 3,700
      Master's Degrees 1,500
      Doctor's Degrees 700

Chapter III

How Do I Know If I Should Be A Scientist?

Choosing a career in science or mathematics is a process that will take a long time and will be determined by many factors. You will have to carefully analyze your own abilities and interests. You will have to consider the time and expense necessary to obtain the skills and education required for the job. You must realistically evaluate your chances of actually getting hired in the occupation you choose. And you must look into the financial and other rewards that the career can offer.

As you read this section, many questions should come to mind. Ask your science teacher or your guidance counselor to help you. Most students do not spend enough time considering their future employment. Realize, however, that what you do as your job is one of the most important decisions of your life.

What Are My Abilities?

Take a few sheets of paper, go to a quiet place in your house, ask your family to leave you alone for the next half hour, and honestly answer these few questions. Don't just write down the first few thoughts that come into your head. Think for a few minutes before you answer. Try to list as many responses as you can, so that you can fully explore your feelings.

1. What do you really enjoy doing? What makes you happy and full of good feelings? What makes you feel alive?
2. What do you do well?
3. What subjects do you enjoy learning in school? Do not, necessarily, list the ones you do best in, but the ones that you find most interesting. (Try to leave out the personalities of your teachers.)
4. What special interests do you have?
5. If you have to do something eight hours a day, five days a week for most of your adult life, what would you really like to do?

6. What do you want to avoid in a job? What are some of the things you don't want to do at work?
7. What are some of the things you don't like to do?
8. What subjects (not teachers) in school do you really hate?
9. What special talents do you have?
10. Close your eyes and for about five minutes daydream about how you would like your life to be. Briefly describe your ideal life.

This self-help inventory should give you some insight into what you want out of life and what your interests are.

Should I Be a Scientist?

Answer the following questions with Yes or No:

1. Am I good at solving mathematical puzzles?
2. Do I know how a lot of things work (like a car, a TV, a toaster)?
3. Can I read a map easily?
4. Do I like watching nature and science shows on TV?
5. Do I like games with lots of rules?
6. Do I like to use tools?
7. Do I like science and natural history museums?
8. If I have a problem, do I prefer figuring it out myself to having somebody else give me the answer?
9. Do I like working by myself?
10. Do I like working with others?
11. Do I have the patience to do something many times until I get it right?
12. Do I like challenges?
13. Do I like mysteries or mysterious ideas?
14. Do I get satisfaction just from doing something well, or do I always need praise or a reward for a job well done?
15. Do I like to study?
16. Can I work in an unstructured situation?
17. Do I ask a lot of questions until I understand a problem or a new idea?
18. Do I sometimes challenge the ideas and attitudes of others?
19. Do I like science courses?
20. Do I like math courses?
21. Do I finish what I start?
22. Money is not the only reason for a job.
23. One of the main reasons I go to school is because I like to learn.
24. I do well in school.
25. Sometimes I like to sit quietly and think.

If most of your answers were Yes, then, perhaps, you should be a scientist.

How Can I Find Out More About Being a Scientist or Mathematician?

Probably the very best way to find out about any occupation is to interview people working in the field. Contact the science or math department at a local college or university. Go to the Yellow Pages and find out if there is a local association of scientists in your community. Call them up. They will be glad to help. Call or write to a local research institution or hospital and ask if you can arrange a visit. Most school districts have annual Career Nights, at which you have the opportunity to talk to people from many different occupations. Take advantage of all of these opportunities.

When you find someone, ask them: What's your job like? Tell me what you do in a typical day? What do you like best about your job? What do you like least? What made you decide to be a scientist? What are the prospects for employment in your field? What kind of training do you need? You can even ask them personal questions that might help to answer some of your concerns, such as: Suppose I'm just pretty good in school. Will that affect my chances of entering your field? Can I be a mother and still work in your field? Do you ever do anything really exciting?

Another good way to find out about occupations is to write to the professional organizations. At the end of each career chapter, I have suggested some places to write. For general information about science careers you should go to your library and ask for a copy of the *Occupational Outlook Handbook* published by the Bureau of Labor Statistics. These volumes tell you about many occupations. There are also several encyclopedias and dictionaries of science and technology, as well as reference works on career and vocational choices, which have entries on science occupations.

A university or college library may have more specialized material such as the publications from the Scientific Manpower Commission and the American Association for the Advancement of Science. Consult the library's catalog for publications by these organizations.

What School Subjects Do I Need to Become a Scientist?

To be a scientist or a mathematician requires an absolute minimum of four years of college leading to a bachelor's degree, and usually a master's degree. In many of the fields, a Ph.D. (Doctor of Philosophy) is required if you want to engage in research or creative work. Some jobs that should not require a doctorate or even a master's degree to perform now have these graduate requirements because so many over-qualified people are seeking employment in that area. Oceanography, for instance, is one of the occupations in which every important scientist has at least one doctorate, and may have two or more.

In high school, prospective scientists and mathematicians should gain as broad a general background as possible in order to qualify for college work. All of the science and math occupations require a basic understanding of biology, chemistry, and physics. Regardless of the field you intend to choose, you should take a year's course in each of these three subjects.

Many students love biology in high school and hope to become life scientists; however, some shy away from taking physics or chemistry because they are afraid that the subjects might be too hard, or that they might require too much math ability, or for some other reason. Avoidance of these courses is very impractical for anyone interested in a career in the life sciences.

Physics is essential for biologists. It is the study of energy. How organisms obtain, store, and use energy is of vital importance in every branch of the life sciences. If you do not comprehend physics, you will not be able to explore the delicate energy transformations that take place between cell and sun, between cell and cell, and between the species of the earth. All of the life functions, such as digestion, circulation, and reproduction, involve physics, as well as the extra-organism studies such as ecology, evolution, animal behavior, and medical sciences.

Chemistry is the study of the components of matter. All living things, being forms of matter and composed of matter, are consequently made up of chemicals. There are thousands of unique chemicals within each living creature. They are in dynamic balance, and each chemical performs a special task. To understand the needs and functions of a flower, a fish, or any life form, the life scientist must know how the chemicals within each organism are formed and how they react. He or she must know chemistry. Therefore, take the basic trio—chemistry, physics, and biology—even if you already know "exactly" which field you want to enter.

In many schools specialty courses such as ecology, oceanography, botany, and laboratory techniques are offered. These science courses are very good to take as electives, or extra courses. However, if you want to be a scientist, *do not* take these courses *instead* of chemistry, biology, or physics. Take them in addition, if you like, but not as substitutes. Colleges require rigorous preparation in science, and often these courses do not meet that requirement.

Courses such as photography, art, drafting, and shop develop very special skills that can give you a special advantage in college, in applying for a job, and on the job as a scientist. They are highly recommended if they can fit into your program.

Mathematics is the foundation of all the sciences. You must take four years of high school mathematics. That means two years of algebra, one year of geometry, and one year of trigonometry. Precalculus, probability theory, statistics, and computer programming will also help you get into college and succeed when you get there. All of these fields are essential for understanding the advanced work carried on in science today. A knowledge of computer programming and statistics is becoming a requirement for almost every college graduate. A tip: Plan to take math in your senior year in high school. Don't "lazy out" of this subject because of "senioritis." If you do not take the course, you might have a much harder time getting started in college.

The need to communicate scientific ideas and discoveries requires good reading, writing, and speaking skills. You should have a good vocabulary and be able to express yourself clearly. High school English and speech courses will help you develop these abilities. Grammar, spelling, and vocabulary are just as important to a scientist as are knowing the parts of the body or knowing arithmetic. Failure to learn these subjects can be a constant embarrassment and can retard your future both in college and on the job. Mastering composition and studying great literature help to train your mind in logical thinking and sensitize your emotions to the feelings of society. With these skills you can analyze and organize your thoughts and your work, and you can carry out research that may be more responsive to the needs of mankind.

Twenty years ago, all physical scientists had to read German and usually one other foreign language in order to keep current in the research literature published in non-English journals. Today, it is not absolutely necessary to have a reading knowledge of foreign languages to succeed in the sciences, since translations of important publications are generally available. However, skill in understanding Russian, Chinese, French, or German is helpful to future scientists and mathematicians. Many works, especially those published before World War II, contain important material but are only available in their original language.

How Good Should My Grades Be If I Want to Become a Scientist?

You need not be a genius to be a competent, productive, successful scientist or mathematician. The competition for jobs is keen, however, and your classwork grades are a good indication of how bright you are *and* how hard you work. Clearly, you should be doing very well in your science classes. You need not be a "straight A" student, but if you are getting a lot of C's in science courses, perhaps your abilities are in other areas. People can love science and can continue to learn about nature while earning a living in a nonscientific occupation. If you are not succeeding at a relatively high level in your science work, think seriously about alternative careers.

A good ability in mathematics is important for a career in the sciences. Not only the physical and environmental sciences, but also the biological and medical fields require a good understanding of advanced mathematics, computer analysis, and statistics. Problem solving, as you do in algebra class, is an important tool for scientific research. Good scientists usually enjoy solving difficult problems, and you should be comfortable with mathematics in order to perform well in your occupation.

Chapter IV

Some Facts About Scientists and Mathematicians

How Much Do Scientists and Mathematicians Earn?

In 1979 the salaries of most scientists and mathematicians were between $20,000 and $50,000 a year. The average salary of scientists is more than twice those of nonsupervisory workers in private industry, except farming. It is almost 25 percent higher than the average salary earned by a professional employee in private industry. In addition, most scientists receive liberal fringe benefits, such as health insurance, paid vacations, paid sick leave, pensions, and free life insurance.

Here is a list of starting salaries for inexperienced scientists in 1978–79.

1978–79 Starting Salaries for Inexperienced Scientists and Mathematicians by Highest Earned Degree*

Field	Bachelor's Degree	Master's Degree	Ph.D.
Agricultural Scientists	$12,552	—	—
Biologists	$12,204	—	—
Chemists	$15,984	$18,624	$24,204
Computer Mathematicians	$16,812	$20,268	—
Mathematicians	$15,888	$18,024	$24,840
Geologists and Earth Scientists	$16,416	$20,208	$25,116
Physicists	$13,836	$17,400	—

* Scientific Manpower Commission, *Salaries of Scientists, Engineers and Technicians,* Washington, D.C., November, 1979.

Experienced scientists, of course, earn considerably more. The following is a list of 1978 salaries for scientists and mathematicians who were working in 1970.

*1978 Average Salaries for Scientists
with 8 Years or More of Experience**

Chemists	$26,700
Physicists/Astronomers	$29,300
Mathematicians	$27,500
Computer Specialists	$25,900
Earth Scientists	$30,600
Oceanographers	$26,800
Meteorologists	$29,700
Biological Scientists	$25,200
Agricultural Scientists	$23,800
Medical Scientists	$28,900

* Scientific Manpower Commission

These figures are a little misleading, however, since people in these fields vary as to average training, average age, and average employer. Generally, Ph.D.'s are paid more than people whose highest degree is a bachelor's degree, even in the same field. That is because scientists with doctorates usually have more responsible positions, supervise several associate or assistant researchers, are more valuable to the company, and so on. In the above figures, the average salary for chemists is considerably lower than the average salary for physicists/astronomers. What is not mentioned is that the average chemist does not have a doctorate, since many jobs in the chemical industry can be had with a bachelor's degree, whereas almost every job in physics or astronomy requires a Ph.D. The average Ph.D. chemist earned $29,000 in 1979, approximately the same as the physicist.

Another confusing factor is age. Generally, as a scientist gains experience, he is better paid. The average meteorologist is about ten years older than the average computer specialist; therefore, the salary differences.

The third factor to consider is the type of employer. Industry usually pays much more than a college or a university. The Federal government usually pays more than a state or local government. Biologists generally are employed by colleges and universities, whereas many earth scientists are employed by oil companies. This should help explain the discrepancies in their salaries.

Below is an interesting table that shows the average salaries of chemists by employer, degree, and sex in 1979.

Scientists' wages also vary according to the money they might make (or save) for their employer, as well as degree of responsibility. Applied researchers, therefore, earn more than basic researchers, and managers earn more than either. Teachers, scientists who work in manufacturing products (not in inventing or discovering them, but in actual production), and scientists who inspect products for safety and purity earn

Median Annual Salaries of Chemists by Type of Employer, Degree Level, and Sex, 1979

Type of Employer	Bachelor's			Degree Level and Sex Master's			Ph.D.'s		
	Men	Women	Total	Men	Women	Total	Men	Women	Total
Industry									
Manufacturing	$25,700	$18,000	$24,700	$28,000	$21,200	$27,000	$33,100	$26,400	$33,000
Non-Manufacturing	23,000	16,400	22,000	25,000	20,300	23,200	31,300	20,200	31,000
Education									
Public University	18,100	11,500	15,300	18,000	15,000	17,600	25,000	18,100	24,500
Private University	11,100	10,700	11,000	16,300	17,600	17,000	23,500	17,400	23,000
High School, Other Schools	13,000	8,800	12,000	16,500	14,600	16,900	19,000	16,000	19,000
Government									
Federal	28,000	24,000	26,000	28,000	19,300	27,000	33,000	28,000	32,000
State/Local	19,400	13,500	18,600	20,000	16,000	19,500	25,000	17,500	24,800
Self-Employment	30,000	—	30,000	36,000	—	36,000	36,000	—	36,000
Hospital/Ind. Lab.	17,000	14,700	17,000	22,400	12,000	22,000	29,000	19,000	29,000
Nonprofit									
Research Inst.	20,000	14,400	18,500	25,000	17,000	22,900	27,600	21,000	27,600
Other	23,000	15,000	21,000	25,000	18,000	23,600	31,000	19,500	30,000

* American Chemical Society, 1979 Survey of ACS Membership Status, June 1979, in Scientific Manpower Commission.

the least. The average experienced scientist in 1978 earned $26,300.

*Average Salaries for Scientists in 1978 by Type of Work**

Production/Inspection Scientists	$25,100
Development/Design Scientists	$25,900
Teachers (also Professors)	$26,100
Basic Researchers	$26,900
Consultants	$27,500
Applied Researchers	$27,800
Managers	$30,800

* Scientific Manpower Commission

Another interesting salary incongruity is evidenced by the average salary of Ph.D. scientists according to type of employer. The average salary of Ph.D.'s in education is only $23,700, nearly 10 percent less than the average salary for all teachers in science (many secondary school science teachers do not have Ph.D.'s and earn more than Ph.D. associate professors). The average salary of Ph.D.'s in the Federal government is $29,700, and the average salary for Ph.D.'s in business and industry is $29,900. The Ph.D. diploma is becoming the prerequisite "working paper" for many jobs in science and mathematics.

A large number of scientists and mathematicians are employed by colleges, universities, community colleges, and secondary schools. Over three-fifths of all life scientists are teachers, over three-fourths of all classical mathematicians, and about one-half of all physicists. Their jobs vary according to their experience, expertise, and institution. In major universities, most science and math faculty teach about 50 percent of the time and carry on basic research the rest. In small colleges and community colleges, more time must be devoted to teaching. In secondary schools, teaching is usually the primary occupation of the scientist. Many scientific faculty supplement their incomes or receive additional "release time" from teaching responsibilities by doing consultant work for the government or for private concerns. Others write textbooks and research articles. Most try to receive grants from the government or from private foundations to support the expenses of their research.

Many scientists feel that the academic life is the most supportive to creative scientific work. Here they work not only with brilliant colleagues but also the brightest graduate students, who are eager to work hard to learn the details of science. At the university they are seldom pressured by the production needs of private industry. They are often allowed the opportunity to pursue basic research topics that further mankind's understanding of nature.

The price that must be paid for academic pursuit is in the pocketbook. The average salary of faculty members in 1978–79 is listed below. As you can see, they earn far less than the average scientist, and virtually all have doctoral-level degrees or training. Young Ph.D.'s usually start their career at a college or university as an assistant professor. If they are very good, after three to five years they will receive tenure (job security). Then they may progress to higher rank. The higher-level positions are usually given to those teachers who have published several original research papers in their fields and are regarded as experts. Tenure, by the way, is very hard to obtain. Many fine scientists do not develop the skills necessary to receive permanent status at a university. They often find work in industry or enter another field.

It must also be added that there are very few openings for science and mathematics teaching faculty. Fewer people are attending colleges and universities, and many institutions are firing instead of hiring.

Salaries of Science and Mathematics Faculty, 1978–79*

Rank	University	4-Year College	2-Year College
Professor	$28,770	$24,650	$21,650
Associate Professor	$21,270	$19,870	$17,460
Assistant Professor	$17,380	$16,500	$14,750

* Scientific Manpower Commission

Deans of science, by the way, earn an average salary of $29,735 in public institutions and $21,714 in private ones.

Secondary school science teaching usually requires a master's degree and special training in education. There are often openings for scientists and mathematicians in public and private high schools and junior high schools, even during times of cutbacks in school budgets. Below is a listing of teaching salaries in public schools throughout the nation. Science teachers, because of their specialized training, often make more than these average salaries. Private schools usually pay less than public ones.

Estimated Average Annual Salary of Elementary and Secondary Public School Teachers by State, 1978–79*

State	Salary	State	Salary
United States	$15,040	Montana	$13,651
Alabama	12,948	Nebraska	12,936
Alaska	24,150	Nevada	15,206
Arizona	15,200	New Hampshire	11,825
Arkansas	11,126	New Jersey	16,325
California	17,580	New Mexico	14,215
Colorado	15,000	New York	18,600

State	Salary	State	Salary
Connecticut	15,235	North Carolina	13,537
Delaware	14,917	North Dakota	12,013
Florida	14,005	Ohio	14,200
Georgia	12,793	Oklahoma	12,498
Hawaii	18,357	Oregon	14,765
Idaho	12,624	Pennsylvania	15,400
Illinois	16,905	Rhode Island	16,698
Indiana	14,194	South Carolina	12,206
Iowa	14,199	South Dakota	11,750
Kansas	12,784	Tennessee	12,733
Kentucky	13,130	Texas	12,975
Louisiana	13,015	Utah	13,910
Maine	12,238	Vermont	11,786
Maryland	16,587	Virginia	13,200
Massachusetts	16,125	Washington	17,400
Michigan	17,974	West Virginia	12,675
Minnesota	15,446	Wisconsin	15,000
Mississippi	11,150	Wyoming	14,469
Missouri	12,896		

* National Education Association, reprinted in *Changing Times,* September 1979.

Perhaps you would like to compare the salaries of scientists with the earnings of other professionals. Here is the latest salary survey by the U.S. Department of Labor.

Average Salaries in Private Industry, March 1979

Accountants, beginning	$13,790
Public accountants, midlevel	$19,174
Auditors, upper level	$20,303
Chief accountants, top level	$45,274
Attorneys, starting	$18,740
Attorneys, high experience	$56,964
Buyers, midlevel	$21,200
Job analysts, upper level	$24,231
Personnel directors, midlevel	$34,285
Chemists, beginning	$14,455
Chemists, upper level	$35,232
Engineers, starting	$17,345
Engineers, top level	$45,221
Engineering technicians, midlevel	$15,094
Drafters, midlevel	$12,835
Computer operators, starting	$ 9,198
Computer operators, top level	$16,975
Accounting clerks, midlevel	$11,367
File clerks, top level	$10,483
Messengers	$ 8,112
Personnel clerks, midlevel	$12,060
Secretaries, beginning	$10,354
Secretaries, top level	$15,693
Stenographers, top level	$12,458
Typists, beginning	$ 8,398

What Is the Average Age of Scientists and Mathematicians?

It is interesting to see which fields have the most young employees. The newer professions, of course, tend to hire the most young employees. The average age of computer specialists in this country in 1976 was 36.9 years. Oceanographers had an average age of 38.9 years. The oldest average age—therefore, we might assume, a harder profession to enter— was for atmospheric scientists, whose average age was 47.9 years.

Average Age for Scientists and Mathematicians (1976)

Computer Specialists	36.9 years
Mathematicians	41.0 years
Life Scientists	43.7 years
Physical Scientists	44.0 years
Environmental Specialists	46.0 years

Are There Many Women Scientists and Mathematicians?

Unfortunately, there are relatively few women in the sciences. About 85 percent or more of the persons in each of the scientific fields are men. The field with the smallest proportion of women is the environmental sciences. The computer, mathematical, and life sciences tend to attract more women, but still the majority of the jobs are filled by men.

Percentage of Males and Females in the Sciences (1976)*

Computer Specialists	87.6% Male and 12.4% Female
Mathematicians	86.5% Male and 13.5% Female
Life Scientists	87.5% Male and 12.5% Female
Physical Sciences	92.5% Male and 7.5% Female
Environmental Sciences	96.8% Male and 3.2% Female

---

* U.S. Department of Commerce, *Selected Characteristics of Persons in Fields of Science or Engineering:* 1976; Series P. 23, #76, October, 1978.

The relatively small number of women attracted to the sciences may be a result of the perception that many women have that science is a job for men. The female's socialization process narrows her career choices and often underutilizes her potential. Most women are employed in low-paying, low-status jobs, where their advancement is restricted. In 1970 half of all working women were employed in only seventeen occupations, chiefly as secretaries, retail sales clerks, bookkeepers, waitresses, and public elementary school teachers.

Why don't women become scientists? Are they denied jobs, or are there just fewer women interested in pursuing science? It is a difficult question. Up to about ten years of age, females have a slight advantage over males because of their early developmental precocity. About the same number of girls like science as boys. By high school age, however, boys are significantly better at science and math than girls, and males tend to like science more than females do. Apparently, our society directs boys toward science and nature, and girls away. Boys are supported and encouraged when they take things apart, play with motors, collect frogs, experiment with rockets, and so on. Girls are not pushed along these lines. Whether they are not initially interested in these things, or whether it is something learned is not clear. However, the results are clear. Nearly 100 percent of all nurses are female, but only 7 percent of doctors are women. Most dental hygienists are female, and most dentists are male. Ninety-nine percent of all engineers are men. Talented women have typically not been encouraged to develop and use their gifts in a technical career.

The situation of narrow career choice is changing radically. More and more women are deciding on full-time careers throughout their adult lives. As women recognize that they will probably be employed at some job for over twenty-five years, they will turn toward jobs that are more interesting and fulfilling. About 7 percent of physicians are female, but nearly 20 percent of all physicians in training are women. Slightly less than 1 percent of engineers are women, but about 5 percent of engineering students are female.* Similar dramatic increases in the proportion of women in all the sciences point the way to a time when greater equality will be found. When more women are scientists we can expect new discoveries that will help push "mankind" toward a greater understanding of the universe.

The National Research Council has reported that the proportion of doctorates granted to women has risen from 13.5 percent in 1970 to 26.9 percent in 1978. While the total number of doctorates (for both males and females) remained about the same in 1978 as in 1971, the number granted to women increased by 80.9 percent during those years.

The survey also shows that the proportion of women doctorate degree holders in the physical sciences, mathematics, and engineering who were actually offered jobs in their profession increased from 36 percent in 1977 to 46 percent in 1978.

Proportion of Doctorates in the Sciences Awarded to Women, 1968, 1978*

	1968		1978	
Field	Total	% Women	Total	% Women
Physics/Astronomy	1,422	2.3	1,066	4.9
Chemistry	1,782	7.8	1,545	12.7
Mathematics	970	4.9	838	14.3

* These statistics are from Walter S. Smith and Kala M. Stroup, *Science Career Exploration for Women,* National Science Teachers Association, 1978.

| | 1968 | | 1978 | |
Field	Total	% Women	Total	% Women
Earth Sciences	438	2.5	623	9.8
Computer Sciences	—	—	121	9.1
Engineering	2,833	0.4	2,423	2.2
Biological Sciences	2,608	17.1	3,192	25.5
Agricultural Sciences	677	1.0	1,012	6.9
Medical Sciences	396	13.6	683	28.8
Psychology	1,452	22.8	3,049	36.8
Social Sciences	1,842	11.5	3,404	24.3
All Sciences/Engineering	14,420	8.9	17,956	19.6
All Fields	22,834	12.7	30,850	26.9

* National Research Council, *Summary Report 1978 Doctorate Recipients from United States Universities*, 1979.

The salaries of women in science average about 20 percent lower than for men. Below is a table comparing average salaries for experienced men and women scientists in 1978.

1978 Average Salaries for Scientists with 8 or More Years' Experience*

Occupation	Males	Females
All Professions	$27,400	$22,600
Chemists	28,000	22,000
Physicists/Astronomers	29,300	30,700
Mathematicians	28,000	22,500
Other Physical Scientists	29,100	Too few positions
Statisticians	27,600	26,700
Computer Specialists	26,200	23,600
Earth Scientists	30,800	24,700
Oceanographers	26,800	Too few positions
Atmospheric Scientists	29,700	Too few positions
Biological Scientists	25,800	21,800
Agricultural Scientists	23,900	Too few positions
Medical Scientists	30,200	22,800

* Scientific Manpower Commission.

The ominous remark "Too few positions" refers to the statistical nature of the table. If fewer than twenty women were surveyed (or found) by the National Science Foundation employed in that occupation for the last eight years, no entry could be made.

As you can see, women scientists are paid much less than males. You may want to argue that the table may be biased by the fact that, proportionately, more men scientists have higher degrees than women. Here is a table that compares salaries by highest degree earned. Still, men earn considerably more than women. At the highest level of education, the Ph.D., you might think that the caliber of professional would outweigh any bias. But male Ph.D.'s earn 20 percent more than their female counterparts.

1978 Average Salaries for Scientists with 8 or More Years' Experience by Highest Earned Degree*

	Males	Females
Bachelor's Degree	$26,600	$22,100
Master's Degree	$27,800	$21,500
Doctor of Philosophy	$30,100	$24,300

* Scientific Manpower Commission

The average women Ph.D. earns $2,300 a year less than the average male professional scientist with only a bachelor's degree.

These statistics, of course, might reflect some historical mistreatment of women professionals. Let us, then, examine some salary and job data gathered by the College Placement Council regarding men and women recently graduated from college. They investigated the job offers made to people who received bachelor's degrees during the academic year 1978–1979. The table includes the percentage of the offers made to men versus the percentage made to women. It also lists the average salaries offered. The first seven occupations are in the sciences and mathematics, the next four are in nonscience professional fields, and the last two are for engineering graduates. The last column in the list compares the number of job offers in 1978–1979 to the number of offers made in 1977–1978. "Down" means there were fewer offers in 1978–1979 than in the previous year. "Up" means there is an improvement in job offers from the previous year.

One of the primary reasons that women professionals earn less than men is the employer they "choose" to work for. Industry and the Federal government pay the highest salaries, while educational institutions and nonprofit organizations pay the least. The following table illustrates the disparity. Curiously, the Federal government has such strong antidiscrimination hiring procedures that a woman applicant has a good chance of landing a job for which she is qualified. Still, women prefer jobs in the fields that pay the least and, coincidentally, offer them the least opportunity for advancement.

Salaries Offered to B.S. Degree Candidates in Technical Careers, 1978–1979*

Employer	Offers to Men (%)	Offers to Women (%)	Average Salary Offered to Men	Average Salary Offered to Women
Business	74	26	$14,604	$13,896
Federal Government	87	13	$15,648	$14,532

A Study of 1978–1979 Salary Offers to B.S. Degree Candidates*

Occupation	Offers to Men (%)	Offers to Women (%)	Average Salary Offered to Men	Average Salary Offered to Women	Comparison to 1977–1978
Agricultural Scientists	83	17	$12,768	$11,484	Down
Biological Scientists	57	43	$12,576	$11,700	Down
Chemists	62	48	$16,080	$15,828	Up
Computer Specialists	66	34	$16,932	$16,572	Up
Mathematicians	55	45	$16,080	$15,648	Up
Medical Scientists	20	80	$16,284	$13,248	Down
Other Physical and Earth Scientists	84	16	$16,560	$15,648	Down
Accounting	68	32	$14,460	$14,484	Up
Business	70	30	$13,332	$12,984	Up
Humanities	39	61	$12,276	$11,484	Down
Economics	64	36	$13,636	$13,200	Down
Electrical Engineering	93	7	$18,216	$18,552	Up
Chemical Engineering	77	23	$19,680	$19,776	Up

* The College Placement Council, A Study of 1978–79 Beginning Offers, Final Report, July, 1979.

Employer	Offers to Men (%)	Offers to Women (%)	Average Salary Offered to Men	Average Salary Offered to Women
State and Local Government	86	14	$14,364	$13,608
Manufacturing/ Industrial	86	14	$18,336	$18,324
Nonprofit and Educational Organizations	26	74	$14,364	$12,588

* College Placement Council.

An Advertising Council poster had a slogan that stated, "Who says that the person who discovers the cure for cancer will be a white man?" The problems of society need the application of gifted minds from both sexes and from all races. Perhaps, because of lack of encouragement and because of discriminatory practices and feelings, a forty-year-old housewife is folding clothes who, in a more enlightened time, could have discovered a cheap, renewable, and pollution-free energy source. Hopefully, for our nation's sake, this trend is changing.

What is the Racial Makeup of the Science Professions?

In 1976 whites accounted for 93 percent or more of the persons in each of the science fields. The proportion of blacks ranged from under 1 percent for environmental scientists to nearly 4 percent for mathematical specialists. The proportion of Orientals ranged among the fields from under 1 percent to about 3 percent.

Races of Scientists and Mathematicians (1976)*

Computer Specialists	96.3%	White	1.6%	Black	1.3%	Oriental
Mathematicians	93.2%	White	3.8%	Black	2.5%	Oriental
Life Scientists	96.2%	White	1.4%	Black	1.7%	Oriental
Physical Scientists	94.3%	White	1.6%	Black	3.3%	Oriental
Environmental Specialists	98.1%	White	0.1%	Black	1.4%	Oriental

* U.S. Department of Commerce.

The discrimination against nonwhites in the science professions is usually passive today. It is not that organizations do not want to hire blacks (as was the case before 1960); it is mainly that few blacks and Hispanics have attained the high level of skills and education required by many of the scientific occupations.

In fact, qualified minority candidates are actively sought and are often offered attractive positions in companies so that a more equitable ratio of races can be established. Most science today is a team effort, and many companies realize that people with different backgrounds and experiences can enrich the working environment so that greater productivity and originality can occur.

As with women, the fact that more minority students are being encouraged to study science and mathematics will produce more black, Asian, and Hispanic scientists. Some large companies and the Federal government have programs and scholarships that offer financial support for minority underprivileged students who have demonstrated an ability to achieve in science.

In What Parts of the Country Are the Jobs for Scientists and Mathematicians?

Most scientists and mathematicians live and work either in the Northeast or the South, with the notable exception of the environmental sciences, which have most of their jobs in the South and West.

Places of Residence for Scientists and Mathematicians (1976)*

	Northeast	North-Central	South	West
Total Adult Population of U.S.	25%	26%	32%	18%
Computer Specialists	31.7%	19.7%	27.8%	19.9%
Mathematicians	22.5%	20.8%	36.7%	18.8%
Life Scientists	18.6%	26.0%	30.6%	24.0%
Physical Scientists	30.7%	23.4%	25.8%	18.7%
Environmental Specialists	10.1%	10.2%	45.5%	32.9%

* U.S. Department of Commerce

Science and mathematics require the combined talents of many persons. Thus, most (as many as 75 to 85 percent of the persons in nearly every field) lived in or near large cities where such pools of talent are generally available. The one exception are the life scientists. This category includes agricultural scientists, so about 40 percent of life scientists live in rural communities. Few American scientists and mathematicians work outside of the country.

Residential Patterns of Scientists and Mathematicians (1976)*

	Metropolitan Areas	Nonmetropolitan Areas
Total Adult Population of U.S.	68%	32%
Computer Specialists	85.1%	14.9%
Mathematicians	75.9%	24.1%
Life Scientists	57.4%	42.6%
Physical Scientists	78.5%	21.5%
Environmental Specialists	77.4%	22.6%

* U.S. Department of Commerce

As you can see, you will have to learn to enjoy urban life if you want to enter the sciences. Some cities, too, especially attract large populations of scientists. Washington, D.C., for example, with its concentration of government employment, has approximately 11 percent of the mathematicians in the country, although it contains only about 1.4 percent of the total population. Denver, Colorado, and Houston, Texas, have, respectively, 7 and 9 percent of all environmental specialists. And New York City has 7 percent of the nation's computer specialists.

How Stable Is Employment in the Sciences and Mathematics?

Unemployment among scientists and mathematicians is very low. Over 98 percent of them had jobs in 1976.

Unemployment Percentages Among Scientists and Mathematicians (1976)*

Computer Specialists	1.4% unemployed
Mathematicians	1.8% unemployed
Life Scientists	1.5% unemployed
Physical Scientists	1.4% unemployed
Environmental Scientists	0.9% unemployed

These figures, however, do not mean that all scientists and mathematicians are employed in science and mathematics. Many have had to find employment in related fields or, sometimes, in quite different occupations. However, the training and education required to make a scientist are well appreciated by employers. Therefore, virtually anyone with a degree in science can find interesting work.

The National Science Foundation predicts that jobs will be available for all work-seeking Ph.D.'s in 1987. However, many may have to take employment in nonscience fields. In 1977 only about 9 percent of the people with doctorates in science held nontraditional jobs. By 1987, the Foundation predicts, about 17 percent will be finding jobs outside their area of expertise.

Chapter V

How Can I Prepare for a Career In Sciences?

While you are in high school, of course, you should be taking the necessary academic subjects to ensure that you can go to college. In addition, many communities have organizations for secondary school students interested in science. Ask your science teacher if there is a Junior Academy of Sciences in your city. Find out if your local zoo or state forest or museum has a youth program. Join an astronomy or rocket club. Your local "Y" may have programs. Many hospitals have special programs where students can assist physicians, nurses, and clinical laboratory workers. You should *actively* seek opportunities that will enrich your understanding of science and provide you with experience in the field. Don't wait for your teacher or your mother to suggest something for you to do; find out for yourself what is available, and sign up.

How Can I Choose a College?

Selecting a college is a very important decision. You should really research a college before enrolling. Find a school that offers the program in which you are interested and in which you can succeed, that you can afford, and at which you have a reasonably good chance of being accepted. If you choose the wrong school, you may have to transfer, losing time, money, and credits; drop out; or flunk out.

At the end of each career chapter in the second half of this book, you will find a brief list of colleges that offer degrees in the various scientific and mathematical careers. For some careers, such as oceanography, only a few colleges offer degrees, while for other careers, such as chemistry, hundreds of institutions have programs. So first, find out what schools offer the career program you want.

Your high school guidance counselor is the best source of information for picking a college. The counselor can tell you about the various colleges and which ones are suitable for you. See your guidance counselor when you are a sophomore. Don't wait until the last half of your junior or the beginning of your senior year. The counselor can tell you what courses to take, what examinations are required, and how to make application.

Colleges pick students by analyzing their academic records, their Scholastic Aptitude Test scores, their achievement and Regents test scores, their personal histories, and their teachers' recommendations. The better these are, the better the school that will accept you.

Reference books, such as *Barron's Profiles of American Colleges and Universities,* give a good sampling of the type of student each college is looking for. If you have trouble with standardized tests, find out if a local community college or other institution offers a course in how to improve your test-taking ability. These courses are helpful to many students. Membership in professional organizations and work in assisting scientists or physicians are valuable experiences that colleges appreciate. A good recommendation from your chemistry, physics, or math teacher is, of course, more valuable for a career in science than one from your gym or social studies teacher.

After you have selected a few colleges, plan to visit them. Write to the admissions office of the college and ask for an interview. Try to get a "feel" for the college. Talk to some of the students on campus. Ask if you can "sit in" on a science lecture. Inspect the laboratories and the other facilities where you will be learning and living. Find out what your program will be like for the next four years. Get the names, from your high school, of students who are attending the colleges in which you are interested. Write to them and find out how they are doing.

Cost is often a determining factor in choosing a college. In general, state- and city-supported institutions are less expensive than private ones. Write to the financial aid office of the colleges to find out what scholarships and loans are available.

Try to find a college that offers an environment in which you feel comfortable and a program where you can master the field of science or mathematics in which you want to work.

How to Choose a Major

In each of the career chapters, there is specific information about college coursework for the various professions. However, early specialization is generally not a good idea. Some fields have so few jobs, such as meteorology or forestry, that a major in one of them may greatly limit your chances of finding a job. Most specialization should take place in graduate school. The best undergraduate majors are those that provide you with the most opportunities as your interests and the needs of the scientific enterprise change. I suggest that you choose a major that leads to a bachelor's degree in chemistry, physics, biology, or mathematics. With one of these degrees you can go to graduate school, medical school, or find a job in hundreds of different fields. A degree in biology with some coursework in agronomy may get you a job in forestry, soil science, range or soil conservation, microbiology, agricultural science, or many other fields; whereas a person with a degree in forestry is very limited in the jobs he or she can find.

How Can I Discover Which Field Is Right for Me?

The rest of this book is divided into chapters that explore many of the major professions in science and mathematics. You will find information about the nature of the work in that occupation, the places that offer employment, the training required, the outlook for jobs, and the earnings and working conditions. You will also find resources for further investigation and a list of colleges that offer programs in the specific field. Use this information as a starting point. It should help you narrow your choices, but don't make a firm commitment until you have discussed your findings with your parents, your teachers, and your guidance counselor. Try to find out more about the profession by writing to the professional organizations and by interviewing people in the field.

Chapter VI

The Physical Sciences: Astronomy, Chemistry, Physics

ASTRONOMY

Astronomy is the study of the sun, the moon, the planets, and the stars, as well as all the intergalactic material of the universe. Astronomers, who are sometimes called astrophysicists, try to answer such questions as:

What is the nature of the atmosphere and surface of Titan, a moon orbiting the planet Saturn?
How does a star form from interstellar dust?
What processes occur on the sun to produce its enormous energy?
What cataclysm causes the collapse of a star into a black hole?
Is there life in outer space?

Unlike other scientists, astronomers cannot experiment with the objects they study. Their laboratory is the universe, and their observations are made from immense distances. Aside from some moon rocks and meteorites, astronomers must get their information from electromagnetic radiation traveling from the vastness of space.

Electromagnetic radiation is emitted from objects that "shine," such as stars (our sun is a star), or are reflected by nonluminous objects, such as planets, moons, or asteroids. Electromagnetic radiation consists of ordinary light, high-energy gamma or X-rays, ultraviolet ("tanning") radiation, infrared (heat) radiation, and radio radiation.

Until the twentieth century, astronomers could detect only the visible light from astronomical bodies. Huge optical telescopes have been built to detect the light that the earth receives from objects in space. This light, however, is very meager. Often the eye, even with the largest telescope, cannot see distant, faint stars. Instead, astronomers use photographic film to record the heavens. Time-exposure photographs increase the brightness of objects invisible to the eye.

An instrument called a spectrograph separates the various colors of starlight so that scientists can determine the chemical constituents of the stars. The element helium was first discovered in 1868 by astrophysicists examining the spectral lines of the sun. Twenty-five years later, helium was found on the earth.

Visible light astronomy gave astrophysicists only an incomplete picture of the universe. Today, astronomers make observations using all parts of the electromagnetic spectrum. Disc-shaped radio telescopes have detected signals from pulsars and quasars that were unknown to optical observers. These vast sources of energy may be the most distant objects in the universe. Infrared astronomy has isolated clouds of dust and gas that are on their way to becoming stars. X-ray spectrographic studies, which must be performed in high-altitude aircraft and spacecraft, have revealed neutron stars and black holes. These black holes, which are located in double star systems, are so dense that not even light can escape their gravitational pull.

What Does an Astronomer Do?

In the past, astronomers usually spent their lives on a mountaintop far from the glow of city lights observing the heavens through their telescopes and examining the photographic plates each day. This is no longer the case. Astronomers now usually live in or near large cities that are convenient to the university or government laboratory that employs them. They spend very little time looking through telescopes. Their observations are made by electronic devices. Their days are usually spent working with a computer in order to add some understanding of the nature of the universe.

A significant amount of an astronomer's time is spent reading the literature that describes other scientists' findings. Time is spent, too, designing and writing research proposals requesting funds from government or private foundations that can support additional research programs. And time is used for travel to distant observatories, conferences, and meetings with other professionals who can aid the astronomer's studies.

Astronomers spend months developing the ideas and designing the equipment they will need to carry out their particular study in space. Usually only a few weeks are spent gathering data at the observatory. The huge telescopes and antennas, in fact, are most often operated by specially trained technologists. More and more data is being obtained from space stations, such as Skylab, and from unmanned satellites that orbit the earth and travel to distant corners of the universe.

An astronomer's research often centers around mathematical concepts derived from the laws of physics. The astrophysicist might, for instance, be interested in studying the effect of a star's gravity on light, or be concerned with the wiggle in a planet's orbit, which could signify the presence of an unseen moon or a more distant planetoid.

Astronomers usually work in teams. The team plans a research program involving measurements and observations that will give clues that may help them understand this aspect of nature. Initially the scientists will study all of the research that has been carried out on the subject. Then they will decide which stars or objects should be studied to gain the information they seek. The next step involves the selection of the instruments and method to be used in making the observation. Often, the astronomers have to devise and construct the equipment they need.

Once the problem, equipment, and methodology have been developed, the team can request a particular telescope or antenna for a specified period of time. Faint optical readings must done on clear, moonless nights. Solar measurements must be performed in daylight. Some readings can be carried out only in airplanes above the atmosphere; others must be gathered in outer space from instruments aboard satellites and rockets.

After the observations have been made, the astrophysicists must analyze the data and determine if the results support their theory. All astronomers use computers to help them make sense of the millions of bits of information they obtain from their observations. The modern computer allows them to make calculations in a few minutes that would have taken years to compute only a decade ago. Even with the modern technologies, the data, which may have taken only an evening to gather, might require months or years to be completely analyzed. Most of an astronomer's time, as you can see, is spent studying and computing. Little time is spent looking through telescopes at the wonders in the heavens.

After the results have been carefully concluded, the astronomers publish their data in scientific journals so that their work will be available for other scientists to use.

An Example of an Astronomical Experiment

Most astronomical studies involve the investigation of a fundamental law of physics. In 1916 Albert Einstein proposed in his general theory of relativity that light energy has an infinitesimal mass which, though unaffected in everyday observations, should be slightly attracted by the huge gravity of the sun. Astronomers were, of course, fascinated by this revolutionary idea. They rushed to be the first to determine if the theory was true.

The theory held that a light ray passing near a massive body, such as the sun, will not appear to travel in a straight line, but will be deflected very slightly (1.74 seconds of arc) toward the body. To test this theory, astronomers had to determine the position of a star at two different times of the year. One reading would be made when the starlight had to go past the sun to reach the earth, and the other at a time when the star was in a position in the heavens far from the sun. The only problem is that stars cannot be seen when the sun is between us and them. There is, however, one time when this observation can be made—at the time of a total eclipse of the sun.

Two British expeditions were dispatched to determine the position of several celestial objects during the eclipse on May 29, 1919. One went to West Africa, and the other to Brazil. Their results confirmed the predictions of the theory. Recent experiments have been performed that tend to show a similar deflection of radio waves from quasars as they pass the sun.

Where Are Astronomers Employed?

Astronomy is the smallest physical science; only 2,000 persons worked as astronomers in 1976. Most professional astronomers are employed as faculty members in colleges or universities. Astronomers in these positions teach, do research, and perform administrative duties. The teaching responsibility of a professor of astronomy differs at each college, but many enjoy teaching introductory astronomy courses to nonscience majors, as well as their specialty courses to advanced astronomy majors. Since physics and mathematics are strongly emphasized in astronomy, some astronomers teach these courses, too, especially at smaller institutions.

A large number of astronomers, 600 in 1976, were employed by the Federal government. Most worked for the National Aeronautics and Space Administration (N.A.S.A.), where they worked on gathering and examining data from manned and unmanned space probes. Other Federal astronomers worked for the Department of Defense, mainly at the U.S. Naval Observatory and the U.S. Naval Research Center. A few Federal astrophysicists are employed by the National Bureau of Standards. Most of these Federal jobs are located near Washington, D.C.

Many astronomers are employed by observatories funded by the Federal government but operated by independent corporations, often associated with universities. These observatories include the Arecibo Observatory, the Cerro Tololo Observatory (in Chile), the Lincoln Laboratory, the Los Alamos Laboratory, the National Center for Atmospheric Research, the National Radio Astronomy Observatory, and the Sacramento Peak Observatory. Many of these facilities are located in isolated Western states, where recordings can be made relatively undisturbed by city lights.

A few astronomers find employment at planetariums, science museums, and astronomy magazines. These scientists spend most of their time improving the general public's interest in and understanding of astronomy. Many public school systems are currently developing astronomy programs for their elementary and secondary school curricula. Some jobs are available with them for astronomers who like working with young people.

Industries, particularly those involved in aerospace government contracts, occasionally hire astronomers to help in the design of instrumentation for space missions.

How Can I Become an Astronomer?

The usual requirement for a job in astronomy is a Ph.D. degree. Almost all teaching and research positions in astronomy are open only to those with the doctorate. A prospective astronomer should be skilled in physics and mathematics and must be able to program computers. He or she should be interested in understanding nature on an exact, quantitative level, enjoy working for days and months on a particular problem, and have the perseverance to endure the years of schooling required for employment.

A few astronomers work in high-altitude aircraft or on top of 14,000-foot mountains, but most spend their days in offices in or near large cities. About 9 percent of all Ph.D. astronomers are women, the highest percentage in the physical sciences, with most holding faculty positions at colleges and universities. There are few minority astronomers, but several black and Hispanic students are pursuing coursework that will lead to professional appointments.

Professional astronomy is usually a course of study only for graduate students. The background for application to a graduate program normally requires a bachelor's degree in the physical sciences or mathematics. A typical candidate would have taken:

a) in high school—biology, chemistry, physics, advanced algebra, geometry, trigonometry, and, often, two years of a foreign language.
b) in the freshman and sophomore years of college—differential and integral calculus, linear algebra, physics (mechanics, heat, sound, electricity, magnetism, atomic theory, light, and optics), English composition, and foreign language.
c) in the junior and senior years of college—advanced physics (including thermodynamics, statistical mechanics, and nuclear structure), advanced differential equations, complex variables, statistics, and computer programming.

The astronomy major may take courses in celestial mechanics, radio astronomy, galactic structure, astrophysics, and kinetic theory.

In graduate school, the astronomy student takes specific courses in his or her area of specialization and begins an astronomy research project, under the supervision of the graduate faculty, culminating in the Ph.D. dissertation.

The master's degree is less important in astronomy than it is in some other fields. It generally involves one or two years of graduate study and may include a thesis or oral examination. It can be a useful credential for members of a technical support staff or for a few positions in planetariums, industry, community colleges, and public schools.

Are There Any Astronomy Jobs That Do Not Require Advanced Degrees?

In many observatories and in some large university laboratories there are positions for persons who are interested in astronomy but do not have graduate school training. These jobs support the research work taking place at the institution. Astronomical research organizations require many highly skilled technical staff members to assist the astrophysicists in their studies. There are opportunities for telescope operators, instrument makers, opticians, electronics technicians, programmers, photographers, and laboratory technologists. Persons so employed work directly with the astronomers and contribute to our knowledge of the universe.

What Are My Chances of Getting a Job as an Astronomer?

Persons seeking jobs as astronomers will face keen competition for the few available openings expected through the mid-1980's. It is estimated that there will only be about 40 new openings a year for astronomers, because the funds available for research, which come mainly from the Federal government, are not expected to increase enough to create new positions. Each year more people receive doctorates in astronomy than there are new openings. Therefore, only the most talented graduates are able to find jobs as astronomers. Others find work teaching related subjects such as physics, meteorology, and computer science, or pursue careers in other science fields.

How Much Do Astronomers Earn?

Astronomers have relatively high salaries. The average salary of an astronomer in 1978 was $29,300. Astronomers with the Ph.D. started in the Federal government in 1978 at $24,703. The average salary for an astronomer in the Federal government in 1978 was $34,715. However, there were only 510 men and 3 women employed as astronomers by the U.S. government during that year. An astronomy professor began at about $17,000 in 1978 and a full professor of astronomy earned about $28,000. A beginning astronomer with a doctorate in 1978 could have earned from $18,000 to $24,000, depending on the employer.

Where Can I Obtain Training in Astronomy?

Some of the colleges and universities that offer a major in astronomy or physics-astronomy are:

Allegheny College, Meadville, Pennsylvania 16335
Amherst College, Amherst, Massachusetts 01002
Bates College, Lewiston, Maine 04240
Bennington College, Bennington, Vermont 05201
Boston University, Boston, Massachusetts 02167
Brown University, Providence, Rhode Island 02912
Bucknell University, Lewisburg, Pennsylvania 17837
Butler University, Indianapolis, Indiana 46208
Carleton College, Northfield, Minnesota 55057
Case Western Reserve University, Cleveland, Ohio 44106
Catawba College, Salisbury, North Carolina 28144
University of Chicago, Chicago, Illinois 60637
University of Cincinnati, Cincinnati, Ohio 45221
Coe College, Cedar Rapids, Iowa 52402
Colgate University, Hamilton, New York 13346
Connecticut College, New London, Connecticut 06320
University of Connecticut, Storrs, Connecticut 06268
Dartmouth College, Hanover, New Hampshire 03755
University of Delaware, Newark, Delaware 19711
Denison University, Granville, Ohio 43023
University of Denver, Denver, Colorado 80210
Dickinson College, Carlisle, Pennsylvania 17013
University of Florida, Gainesville, Florida 32611
Franklin and Marshall College, Lancaster, Pennsylvania 17604
Georgetown University, Washington, D.C. 20007
Goucher College, Towson, Maryland 21204
Harvard University, Cambridge, Massachusetts 02138
Haverford College, Haverford, Pennsylvania 19041
University of Houston, Houston, Texas 77004
University of Illinois, Urbana, Illinois 61801
Indiana University, Bloomington, Indiana 47401
University of Iowa, Iowa City, Iowa 52242
Johns Hopkins University, Baltimore, Maryland 21218
University of Kansas, Lawrence, Kansas 66045
Lehman College, C.U.N.Y., New York, N.Y. 10031
Longwood College, Farmville, Virginia 23901
University of Massachusetts, Amherst, Massachusetts 01002
Michigan State University, East Lansing, Michigan 48823
Mount Holyoke College, South Hadley, Massachusetts 01075
University of Nebraska, Lincoln, Nebraska 68508
Northwestern University, Evanston, Illinois 60201
Notre Dame College, Cleveland, Ohio 44121
Ohio Northern University, Ada, Ohio 45810

Ohio University, Athens, Ohio 45701
University of Oklahoma, Norman, Oklahoma 73069
Pennsylvania State University, University Park, Pennsylvania 16802
Princeton University, Princeton, New Jersey 08540
Purdue University, West Lafayette, Indiana 47907
Rensselaer Polytechnic Institute, Troy, New York 12181
University of Rhode Island, Kingston, Rhode Island 02881
University of Rochester, Rochester, New York 14627
Sam Houston State University, Huntsville, Texas 77340
Smith College, Northampton, Massachusetts 01060
Southern Illinois University, Carbondale, Illinois 62901
Southwestern College, Winfield, Kansas 67156
Swarthmore College, Swarthmore, Pennsylvania 19081
Sweet Briar College, Sweet Briar, Virginia 24595
Vanderbilt University, Nashville, Tennessee 37240
Villanova University, Villanova, Pennsylvania 19085
University of Virginia, Charlottesville, Virginia 22903
Wesleyan College, Middletown, Connecticut 06457
West Virginia University, Morgantown, West Virginia 26506
Williams College, Williamstown, Massachusetts 01267
Wittenberg University, Springfield, Ohio 45501
Worcester Polytechnic Institute, Worcester, Massachusetts 01520

Where Can I Get More Information About Astronomy?

For further information write to:

Education Office
American Astronomical Society
Sharp Laboratory
University of Delaware
Newark, DE 19711

For information concerning Federal employment write to:

Interagency Board of Civil Service Examiners
1900 E Street, N.W.
Washington, DC 20415

For detailed information about careers in astronomy read:

Astronomy Careers, A Definitive Study of Your Future in Astronomy by
Raymond M. Bell. Richards Rosen Press, Inc.

CHEMISTRY

Chemistry is the study of matter and how it changes. The chemist
wants to know what substances are made of, how they react, and how

they change. Chemists are curious about why rubber is soft and why a diamond is hard. Why does iron rust and silver tarnish, but gold stays shiny forever? Chemists have been responsible for the drugs that save lives, as well as for the pollutants that infect our environment. Chemistry is a tremendous industry, employing over half a million people and providing billions of dollars worth of consumer goods that have given our society its style, its comfort, its entertainment, and, regrettably, some of its problems.

Chemistry affects our lives in many ways. When you are sick, the physician prescribes a drug discovered and produced by chemists. Chemical research is responsible for synthetic fibers, plastics, and synthetic rubber used in the tires and other parts of automobiles. Synthetic fertilizers that increase the yield of food from each acre of land were developed in the laboratory. So were the insecticides that prevent the destruction of crops by insects.

The soap and toothpaste you use, as well as your toothbrush, hairbrush, and comb, are products from the chemical industry. Your perfume and your cologne are from the chemical cosmetic factories. If you look at the label on the side of a cereal box, you will discover a list of chemical additives including BHA or BHT, which were invented by chemists to keep the crackle in your puff.

Natural energy resources, such as gasoline, require complex chemical processes to change the thick crude oil into the clear, free-flowing liquid needed by an automobile engine. The car battery, too, is a product of a major branch of the chemical industry.

Today, chemical researchers are busily seeking new energy resources. They are trying to design electrochemical batteries that can run automobiles and supply the current for our houses. And they are trying to develop synthetic fuels so that our country will not be dependent on foreign interests for its energy.

The production of many of these beneficial products, however, has also affected our environment in harmful ways. Poisonous wastes from a chemical plant in Japan found their way into fish living in the nearby waters. Many persons eating the fish died as a result of the poison. Industrial wastes buried near the Love Canal have risen to the surface, endangering the health of the community in New York State. The air around some manufacturing plants contains corrosive acid vapors as a result of industrial pollution. These can damage crops and wildlife and corrode buildings and monuments.

Manufacture of some products has created new and unexpected problems. Lead from the exhaust of automobiles released into the air has been carried all over the earth by currents in the atmosphere. It has even been found in ice at the North Pole. Similarly, fluorocarbons from spray cans are threatening the ultraviolet-light–absorbing ozone layer in the upper reaches of the stratosphere.

Even the manufacture of chemicals intended for beneficial purposes has not been without mishap. A drug called thalidomide, used by some pregnant women to help them sleep, resulted in deformities in their babies. The insecticide DDT nearly caused the extinction of several species of birds, including the bald eagle, our national symbol, before it was banned by law.

Chemists serve an important function in our society. They are well-paid, hard-working people who are trying to improve our lives. Now, through new laws and agencies such as the Environmental Protection Agency and the Federal Drug Administration, chemists are working with the government and with private citizen groups to protect our safety, our health, and our environment.

The Major Branches of Chemistry

Chemistry is divided into many branches that are not clearly distinguished. These branches developed as chemists began to specialize on various problems. There are five basic areas of chemistry: (1) organic chemistry, which is concerned with the chemical compounds that contain carbon; (2) inorganic chemistry, which is the study of the compounds of the other 105 elements; (3) physical chemistry, which studies the physical characteristics of matter and seeks a mathematical explanation of chemical processes; (4) analytical chemistry, which is concerned with determining the composition of substances; and (5) biochemistry, which studies the chemical processes in living things.

There are several occupations within each of these five areas.

Colloid chemistry is the study of materials such as emulsions, fogs, gels, and smokes. *Colloid chemists* are interested in improving aerosol sprays. They are also interested in filters that can separate pollutants from the air and from cigarette smoke. They work with photographic film developing, as well as in the milk industry.

Geochemistry is the study of substances in the earth and the chemical changes they undergo. *Geochemists* often analyze rock and land structures to determine if enough mineral or fuel deposits are present for profitable mining and drilling operations. Geochemists are working with oil companies today to find methods for extracting oil from shale rock and coal. Geochemists also work with archeologists and paleontologists to help us understand what life was like on the earth hundreds, thousands, and millions of years ago.

Polymer chemists are interested in the long chain molecules that are useful in the home and in industry and are the essence of life. Polyethylene is the substance from which plastic bags are made. It is a polymer of ethylene, a light hydrocarbon obtained from the cracking of crude oil. It is relatively unreactive, so it can safely protect food. Other household polymers are teflon, vinyl, nylon, rayon, and dacron. Soap and detergents are polymers, as well as rubber and many pesticides. The long, spiral-staircase molecule DNA, which passes on genetic information from cell to cell, is a polymer, as are hemoglobin, insulin, and other proteins in the body.

Synthetic chemists try to put together simple compounds into complex materials that can be useful to industry and mankind. They make drugs, plastics, paints, food additives, lubricants, fibers, paper products, alloys, and on and on. They are the inventors in the field of chemistry. They

BELL LABS

In materials science research, an experimenter places printed circuits with a new protective coating into an oven to test how they are affected by heat and humidity.

decide on what kind of physical and chemical properties a new substance must have to serve industry or a consumer need; then they set out to construct it in an inexpensive, productive way.

Radiochemists study chemical processess by using radioactive tracer materials. They have examined how drugs and chemicals work in the body, how sewage flows through waste disposal procedures, how oil flows through pipelines, and how oxygen is utilized in the photosynthetic reaction of plants. Rosalyn Yalow won the Nobel Prize for her work on how radioactive tracers can be used for diagnosing medical problems.

Analytical instrumentation chemists are used by industry, by research institutions, and by hospitals to identify and monitor chemical processes with the use of highly accurate instruments. Their instruments can often detect materials in the parts-per-billion range. They can identify what substance may be a causative agent in a disease or if a truly new material has been discovered. In the food industry, they continuously check batches of products for contamination and spoilage.

Agricultural chemists are interested in the chemical processes involved in growing crops. They work in developing fertilizers, weed killers, and insecticides.

Chemotherapy or *medicinal chemists* are involved in the preparation of drugs for treating disease. Medicinal chemists specialize in direct patient care (whereas synthetic chemists are concerned with invention of a drug). They deal with patient dosages and the effects and side-effects of drug therapy. Recent chemotherapy advances have significantly reduced the disability and death rates of many cancers.

Molecular biophysical chemists are involved with trying to explain in mathematical terms the role of molecules and chemical reactions in living things. James Watson and Francis Crick were molecular biophysical chemists who won the Nobel Prize for deciphering the double helix of DNA. These chemists use computer models to help them understand nature's secrets.

Pathological chemists study the chemical effects of disease on the body. They analyze diseased organs and tissues to determine how the chemical balance within the body was upset by the virus, the bacterium, the injury, or the cancer.

Thermochemists study the exchange of energy between a chemical system and its surroundings. They determine whether reactions can occur and at what temperatures and conditions the most product can be formed. Their physical chemical measurements and research are vital to the understanding of how nature recombines atoms to form new molecules.

Metallurgical chemists are concerned with the manufacture of metals and their alloys. They try to develop combinations of metals with other compounds to produce materials with special properties. Anodized aluminum is light, colorful, rust-resistant, and strong. Titanium steel is so hard and strong that it is used in spacecraft designs.

Electrochemists study the generation of electricity in chemical reactions. The dry cell is an example of an electrochemical reaction. Special storage batteries are being developed that can hold the energy generated by solar batteries. Electrochemists are also concerned with corrosion, which involves the transfer of electrons, and with electroplating processes used in industry.

Nuclear chemistry involves the study of radioactive substances. During World War II nuclear chemists were stationed at Columbia University to develop chemical techniques for separating uranium-235, which is fissionable and can be used to make plutonium for an atomic bomb, from uranium-238. Glenn T. Seaborg received the Nobel Prize for heading the research teams that developed the transuranic elements, such as americium, einsteinium, californium, and berklium.

Photochemists study the effect of light on substances. Photography is a chemical reaction that starts when light energy strikes the film. Photochemicals have been developed that can take pictures in virtual darkness, in outer space, and within living organisms. Sixty-second color developing is common. Photosynthesis is a photosynthetic reaction, and so is tanning. These, too, are being investigated by photochemists.

Radiation chemists study the chemical effects of chemical radiation on substances. Radiation can alter inorganic and biological chemical reactions. X-radiation, as well as light from laser radiation, is being

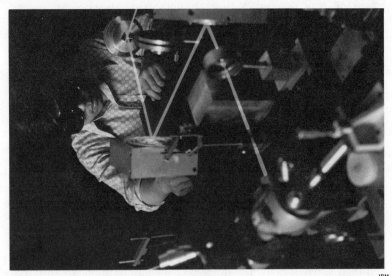

IBM

A scientist at an IBM laboratory in New York explores laser technology.

used to monitor and control chemical reactions. The effect of low-energy radiation from such sources as microwave ovens is being studied by radiation chemists and medical personnel.

Structural chemists are interested in the ways in which atoms link to form molecules. They study crystals and try to develop new materials that have improved properties. One of the current branches of research in structural chemistry involves the production of microchips for computers. These ultrafine crystals have reduced the size of computers from giant room-size devices to calculators that can fit on the face of a watch dial.

Surface chemists study the chemical processes that take place at the surface of liquids and tiny solid particles. Detergents are the most common surface-active materials; however, surfactants are used in the oil and cosmetic industries and in many other fields. Surface chemists study the interfacial reactions that occur across cell membranes and are actively involved in studying reactions that occur when two media are in contact, such as in the production of nylon.

Others careers in chemistry include science writing, forensics (police chemistry), museum work, toxicology, patent law, and chemical sales. Many chemists teach in secondary schools, community colleges, and universities. Many people trained in chemistry deal with the administrative details of funding and managing ongoing research and development projects. The U.S. Army and other military agencies hire chemists to help them with defense, security, and personnel needs. Many chemists also work at manufacturing and industrial facilities implementing new chemical discoveries and techniques into practical products.

Where Are Chemists Employed?

Nearly 150,000 people worked as chemists in 1976. Almost 100,000 of these worked in private industry. About 50,000 worked in companies where chemicals are produced for other industries, and the rest for companies that manufacture food products, scientific instruments, oil companies, paper companies, and electrical equipment concerns.

Colleges and universities employed over 25,000 chemists in 1976. An equal number worked for state and local governments, primarily as agricultural chemists, for public health departments, and for the Federal government. Chemists in the Federal government work for the Department of Defense, the Department of Health and Welfare, the Department of Agriculture, and the Department of the Interior. Many government scientists are involved in regulatory positions. They check whether products meet the safety and health standards established by the government.

Nonprofit research organizations employ chemists to do basic research in such fields as pharmaceuticals, textile chemistry, tobacco research, agricultural chemistry, crystallography, and metallurgy. The research at these facilities is often supported by foundations established by the industries they serve, and their new discoveries are used to produce better and more varied products.

Careers in chemistry are extremely varied. Research chemists work in basic research to learn more about nature. In industry, basic research programs aim at a better understanding of the materials produced by a company. For example, a plastics company will hire a polymer chemist to do basic research in how long chain molecules can be put together with new properties. A drug company may have a group of chemists working at the development of a new drug to combat skin disease. The government might sponsor research in nuclear chemistry, and so on.

Chemistry teachers work in high schools and community colleges, teaching courses both to students interested in becoming chemists and to those who want to learn about an important part of our modern-day technology. Chemistry teaching requires a degree in chemistry as well as special training in teaching techniques.

Chemical salesmen sell chemical products. They help firms select the best products to meet their needs. A chemical salesman needs special training by his company to understand the nature and the uses of the products. Some chemical salesmen specialize in selling advanced electronic equipment used by analytical chemists and for specialized research. These salesmen become experts in their fields and are often sought for their advice and technical know-how during advanced research. Chemical salesmen usually have a minimum of a bachelor's degree in chemistry.

Chemical literature specialists are librarians or technical writers. Chemical librarians help research chemists locate information in books, documents, and other reading materials. Chemical writers may prepare reports or compose training manuals for chemical companies.

Other chemists have used their training in such fields as art preservation, patent law, banking and finance, and as consultants.

The working conditions of most chemists are the same as for most middle-income wage earners. They work 35-hour weeks in well equipped, air-conditioned laboratories. Sometimes, in chemical industry positions, a chemist must work on a night shift to supervise health standards or to monitor the chemical production that goes on around the clock. Occasionally a particular research project requires long hours and weekend work. However, most chemists find these kinds of investigations intriguing and enjoy participating in the act of discovery.

The laboratories and factories they work in are constantly inspected for safety and health hazards. Chemists working with dangerous chemicals are continually examined for ill effects. Those working near radioactive sources wear photographic film badges, which are examined weekly. Every possible precaution is taken to protect workers from immediate or delayed injuries that can result from their jobs. The chemical industry has an excellent safety record.

Chemists are employed in all parts of the country, but most live and work in large industrial areas. Nearly one-fifth of all chemists are located in New York, Chicago, Philadelphia, and Newark. Fifty percent of all chemists work in only six states—New York, New Jersey, California, Pennsylvania, Ohio, and Illinois.

How Can I Become a Chemist?

Chemistry is one of the few scientific professions in which many jobs are available for those with only a bachelor's degree. In fact, if you want to begin your career as a technician, a high school education or an associate's degree is usually sufficient. If you prefer a career with more scientific responsibilities or if you think you would like a supervisory position, you will need a master's degree. Research chemistry and university faculty positions now require a minimum of a Ph.D. degree, and many institutions want job candidates to have postdoctoral training.

One very good quality within the field of chemistry is that many people begin their careers as chemical technicians or chemists with bachelor's degrees and work up to more interesting and challenging positions by acquiring experience and by attending graduate school or college part time. The expenses for your schooling, in fact, are often paid by the company for which you work.

Students planning careers in chemistry should enjoy studying science and mathematics and should like working with their hands building scientific equipment and performing experiments. Perseverance and the ability to concentrate on detail and to work independently are essential. Chemists, too, must be able to work well with other members of their research team, and be able to instruct and inform others who are relying on their results. Other desirable assets include an inquisitive mind and imagination. Chemists also should have good eyesight and good eye-hand coordination, since the careful manipulation of equipment is essential to the job.

In high school, a person interested in becoming a chemist should take at least one course each in biology, chemistry, and physics. If possible, other science courses or, better, advanced placement courses in chemistry will help you toward your career. Mathematics is required for all the physical sciences. You will need three semesters of algebra, plane and solid geometry, trigonometry, and, if possible, precalculus. English and speech are essential because professionals must communicate effectively. Courses that emphasize the study of grammar, writing, term-paper preparation, and journalism will be very useful. If available, a course in public speaking will give you assurance in communicating your ideas and in presenting yourself for college and employment interviews. Two or three years of foreign language study is helpful. German, Russian, or Chinese should be your choice, if available, since many chemistry papers are untranslated or poorly translated from these languages, and much scientific work has been published in journals and books. Social studies are a necessary complement to your coursework, particularly world history and geography.

A bachelor's degree program in chemistry requires at least one chemistry course during each semester. Start with a one-year course in general chemistry and qualitative analysis, then a year's course in organic chemistry and a year's course in physical chemistry, as well as courses in analytical chemistry, biochemistry, and, sometimes, polymer chemistry or inorganic chemistry or both. A chemistry major must also take courses in calculus and, often, advanced mathematics, such as linear equations or matrix algebra. Computer programming is now becoming a requirement for many college degrees.

Chemistry students study university physics as well as college biology. Often, special biology courses such as anatomy and physiology or pharmacology and special physics courses such as quantum mechanics are helpful to those who want to go on for advanced degrees. Chemistry majors must also study general college subjects such as the humanities, social science, fine arts, psychology, economics, pre-law, and communications to round out their studies and prepare them for interesting careers in a changing society. Almost 1,800 colleges and universities offer bachelor's degrees in chemistry.

In graduate school, the chemistry major takes specific courses in the area of specialization as well as advanced physics, biology, mathematics, and computer science. The chemistry student will also begin a chemistry research project under the supervision of the graduate faculty, which will culminate in a master's or doctoral dissertation. Even after the doctorate is received, many chemists spend one or two years as postdoctoral students, learning advanced techniques under the supervision of a prominent researcher. More than 350 colleges and universities offer advanced degrees in chemistry.

Chemical technician jobs do not usually require a bachelor's degree. Instead, an associate degree from a community college can prepare students for many jobs in the chemical industries. In general, chemists who understand the theory of chemical reactions and processes design and plan what chemical technicians operate. Chemical technicians are the experts in the management and operation of the equipment necessary to conduct experiments and to test samples. For example, at a dairy, a chemist may design tests for various milk products. These tests must be carried out on every batch of milk, twenty-four hours a day. The chemical technician is trained to carry out the tests and learns to interpret the results. The technician then performs the needed analyses for the dairy, leaving the chemist free for more difficult tasks. Chemical technology courses at two-year colleges comprise a core of chemistry courses and additional courses in English, speech, psychology, industrial safety, mathematics, and others.

What Are My Chances of Getting a Job as a Chemist?

Employment opportunities in chemistry are expected to be good for graduates at all degree levels through the mid-1980's. Over 6,500 chemistry positions will be available each year. It is expected that the number of positions for chemists will grow within the next ten years from 15 percent to 25 percent over the current level of about 150,000 persons. This could mean over 65,000 new jobs in the next decade. In addition, several thousand openings will result each year as chemists retire, die, or transfer to other occupations. These figures are based on statistics available in the mid-1970's, before the oil crisis of 1979. New research and government funds in the production of synthetic fuels should increase the figures.

Approximately three-fourths of total employment is expected to be in private industry, primarily in the development of new products. In addition, industrial companies and government agencies will need chemists to help solve problems related to the energy shortage, pollution control, and health care.

Few jobs are expected in college and university employment, and the competition will be keen. Some graduates will find jobs as teachers in high schools and in two-year community colleges.

Women and minority group chemists are being particularly sought by chemical companies to make up for the historical disproportion of these groups.

Curiously, the number of people seeking degrees in chemistry has not risen with the demand for chemists. Therefore, jobs are rather easy to come by, especially in the industrial fields, for qualified chemists.

How Much Do Chemists Earn?

Salaries of chemical professionals vary depending on educational background, geographical area, work experience, type of employer, and field of specialization. The American Chemical Society survey of 1979 found that the average starting salary for a chemist with a bachelor's degree was $16,000; for one with a master's degree, $18,600; and for one with a Ph.D., $24,200. The average salary for an experienced chemist in 1978 was $26,700.

In colleges and universities, the average salary of an assistant professor of chemistry was $17,000 in 1979, and the salary for a full professor was $27,000. Professors of chemistry must have a Ph.D. degree. In addition, many experienced chemists in educational institutions supplement their salary with income from consulting, lecturing, and writing.

In 1978 the average salary for all chemists in the Federal government was $27,000 a year. Beginning chemists with bachelor's degrees in 1978 started at $11,243 or $13,925, depending on their college records. Those with master's degrees started at $17,035 or $20,611, and those with doctorates started at $24,703.

Where Can I Obtain Training in Chemistry?

Some of the colleges and universities that offer a major in chemistry are:

University of Akron, Akron, Ohio 44325
University of Alaska, College, Alaska 99701

Antioch College, Yellow Springs, Ohio 45387
Barnard College, New York, N.Y. 10027
Bates College, Lewiston, Maine 04240
Baylor University, Waco, Texas 76703
Boston College, Chestnut Hill, Massachusetts 02167
Brown University, Providence, Rhode Island 02912
Bryn Mawr College, Bryn Mawr, Pennsylvania 19010
Carleton College, Northfield, Minnesota 55057
Carnegie-Mellon University, Pittsburgh, Pennsylvania 15213
The Citadel, Charleston, South Carolina 29409
Clemson University, Clemson, South Carolina 29631
Colby College, Waterville, Maine 04901
Colorado State University, Fort Collins, Colorado 80521
Cornell University, Ithaca, New York 14850
Davidson College, Davidson, North Carolina 28036
Delaware State College, Dover, Delaware 19901
Douglass College, New Brunswick, New Jersey 08102
Drake University, Des Moines, Iowa 50311
Drew University, Madison, New Jersey 07940
Eastern Michigan University, Ypsilanti, Michigan 48197
Fairleigh Dickinson University, Rutherford, New Jersey 07070,
    and Teaneck, New Jersey 07666
Georgia Institute of Technology, Atlanta, Georgia 30332
Gettysburg College, Gettysburg, Pennsylvania 17325
Haverford College, Haverford, Pennsylvania 19041
Hiram College, Hiram, Ohio 44234
Howard University, Washington, D.C. 20001
Illinois Institute of Technology, Chicago, Illinois 60616
Knox College, Galesburg, Illinois 61401
La Salle College, Philadelphia, Pennsylvania 19141
Le Moyne College, Syracuse, New York 13214
Lebanon Valley College, Annville, Pennsylvania 17003
Loyola University, Chicago, Illinois 60611
Manhattan College, New York, N.Y. 10471
Marquette University, Milwaukee, Wisconsin 53233
Marshall University, Huntington, West Virginia 25705
McMurry College, Abilene, Texas 79605
Merrimack College, North Andover, Massachusetts 01845
University of Miami, Coral Gables, Florida 33124
University of Michigan, Ann Arbor, Michigan 48104
Middlebury College, Middlebury, Vermont 05753
University of Mississippi, University, Mississippi 38677
Monmouth College, Monmouth, Illinois 61462
Moravian College, Bethlehem, Pennsylvania 18018
Mount St. Vincent College, Riverdale, New York 10471
Muskingum College, New Concord, Ohio 43762
Nebraska Wesleyan University, Lincoln, Nebraska 68504
University of Nevada, Las Vegas, Nevada 89154

New York University, New York, N.Y. 10003
North Dakota State University, Fargo, North Dakota 58102
Norwich University, Northfield, Vermont 05663
Ohio State University, Columbus, Ohio 43212
University of Oregon, Eugene, Oregon 97403
Pacific Lutheran University, Tacoma, Washington 98447
Philadelphia College of Textiles and Sciences, Philadelphia, Pennsylvania 19104
University of Portland, Portland, Oregon 97203
Providence College, Providence, Rhode Island 02918
Reed College, Portland, Oregon 97202
Rice University, Houston, Texas 77001
Ripon College, Ripon, Wisconsin 54971
University of Rochester, Rochester, New York 14627
Sam Houston State University, Huntsville, Texas 77340
Simmons College, Boston, Massachusetts 02115
University of South Carolina, Columbia, South Carolina 29208
University of South Florida, Tampa, Florida 33620
St. John Fisher College, Rochester, New York 14618
St. Lawrence University, Canton, New York 13617
St. Louis University, St. Louis, Missouri 63103
State University of New York (Albany, Binghamton, Buffalo, Stony Brook, Cortland, Fredonia, Geneseo, New Paltz, Oneonta, Oswego)
Stetson University, Deland, Florida 32720
Swarthmore College, Swarthmore, Pennsylvania 19081
Syracuse University, Syracuse, New York 13210
Texas Christian University, Forth Worth, Texas 76129
Trinity University, San Antonio, Texas 78284
Tufts University, Medford, Massachusetts 02155
Tulane University, New Orleans, Louisiana 70118
University of Tulsa, Tulsa, Oklahoma 74104
Vanderbilt University, Nashville, Tennessee 37240
Vassar College, Poughkeepsie, New York 12601
University of Virginia, Charlottesville, Virginia 22903
Wake Forest University, Winston-Salem, North Carolina 27109
Washington and Jefferson College, Washington, Pennsylvania 15301
Wellesley College, Wellesley, Massachusetts 02181
Wesleyan College, Middletown, Connecticut 06457
Westminster College, Fulton, Missouri 65251
Widener College, Chester, Pennsylvania 19013
College of William and Mary, Williamsburg, Virginia 23185
Williams College, Williamstown, Massachusetts 01267
College of Wooster, Wooster, Ohio 44691
Yale College, New Haven, Connecticut 06520

Where Can I Get More Information About Chemistry?

For further information write to:

The American Chemical Society
1155 16th Street, N.W.
Washington, DC 20036

Manufacturing Chemists Association
1825 Connecticut Avenue, N.W.
Washington, DC 20009

For information concerning Federal employment write to:

Interagency Board of U.S. Civil Service Examiners for Washington, D.C.
1900 E Street N.W.
Washington, DC 20415

PHYSICS

Physics is the science that is concerned with the properties of matter and the laws that describe how energy and matter behave. Physics is the most diverse of all the sciences. Its goal is to describe natural phenomena in the simplest way. Physicists are involved in trying to understand how sounds are made, absorbed, reflected, amplified, and reduced. They study how machines can be made to run more effectively and efficiently. They are interested in light and in ways to focus and amplify its power. They study the way heat and stress affect various materials. Physicists invented the transistor, the Geiger counter, the X-ray machine, the guidance systems for boats, planes, and spacecraft, television, radio, photography, and on and on. Nuclear physicists are exploring the atom for new sources of energy and for a clearer understanding of how all matter is constructed. Some current investigations of physicists are trying to answer these questions:

How can a subway train be made less noisy?
How can a fetus be studied within the womb by sound waves instead of dangerous X-radiation?
What holds the nucleus of an atom together?
What kind of lubricant can keep a wheel on a lunar lander turning while the moon's surface temperature ranges from 260°F to −280°F?
Can a practical design be developed for an electric car?
How is genetic information transferred in a living cell?

The Major Branches of Physics

Solid-state physicists investigate the properties of materials such as metals, alloys, semiconductors, and insulators. They supplied information that led to such developments as the transistor and the solar battery.

Solid-state physics studies the physical properties and atomic structure of solids, particularly of crystals. Research now going on may show how to grow useful-sized single crystals of metals, which would be thousands of times stronger than the best steel available today. Solid-state physicists are also concerned with the relationship between the purity of a metal and its strength and ability to conduct electricity.

Nuclear physicists are interested in the central core of the atom. They use large particle accelerators to smash nuclei in order to discover what they are made of and how they are held together. Nuclear energy is used for defense, in the production of electricity, and in the treatment of cancer. Nuclear physicists are looking for ways to control the tremendous power stored in the atom.

Optical physicists are interested in light—how to produce it, how to control it, and how to understand its nature. Early physicists designed such instruments as the microscope and the telescope. Studies in the colors (spectra) of light given off when a material is vaporized have led scientists to the development of extremely sensitive instruments that can identify minute quantities of substances. Research into lasers has already been applied to everything from eye surgery to cutting tools for the metals industry, and it may in the future lead to the development of triggers for fusion power plants. Many optical physicists are currently engaged in research on finding efficient ways of turning sunlight into electricity and heat.

Atomic and molecular physicists study how the electrons and the nucleus inside an atom interact, and how atoms combine to form molecules. Their work helps the chemists in understanding chemical reactions. The work of atomic and molecular physicists is especially useful in the manufacture of chemicals and pharmaceuticals. They develop new materials, such as ceramics, which can withstand high temperatures and are unbreakable.

Fluid and plasma physicists study the forces and motion of liquids and gases. The plasma physicist is interested in electrically charged fluids, whereas the fluid physicist deals with the flow of uncharged fluids. Fluid physics is essential in the design of streamlined cars, ships, and aircraft and is critical in the production of propulsion systems such as jet engines. The plasmas studied by plasma physicists are produced at high temperatures and are important in the design of reentry space vehicles and in controlling nuclear fusion reactions. At the temperatures of a plasma, new alignments of molecules can occur that may lead to the production of materials with unique properties.

Two of the newer branches of physics are *space* and *planetary physics.* Space physicists study the region between the planets. This near-vacuum area still contains many nuclear particles, atoms, molecules, and meteorites, and it is crossed by various types of radiation from the sun and other cosmic emitters. All of these things must be studied to learn about the history of our world, to protect astronauts and unmanned satellites, and to aid in weather forecasting. Television and telephone communications, as well as the national defense, are relying more and more on satellite relay systems, which can be seriously affected by space particles and radiation. It is the job of the space physicist to help in the design of these expensive satellites in order that they function flawlessly.

Planetary physicists are interested in conditions closer to home. Their studies range from the upper atmosphere to the depths of the ocean. They study the physics of the earth itself. Long-range weather prediction, studies of the migration of fish along ocean currents, the gravitational and magnetic fields of our planet, and exploring for new oilfields involve planetary physics.

Acoustical physicists study sound and its transmission. Their work is applied in the design of great symphonic auditoriums and in the invention of the "invisible" hearing aid. Your stereo tape deck and the ultrasonic scanner used by physicians have been developed from basic research into sound. Many acoustical physicists work in the field of transportation, where they study ways to eliminate or control shock and vibration. Sound navigation systems (sonar), which were developed by acoustical physicists to steer submarines and to detect enemy ships, are now being used to map the ocean bottom and to detect schools of fish. Some acoustical physicists are working with medical scientists in the study of the physiology and psychology of sound and speech communication.

Biophysicists are applying the techniques developed in other branches of physics to biological problems. The physical mechanisms of seeing, hearing, feeling, and thinking are being studied by biophysicists. The effects of X-rays and nuclear particles on cells and tissues are being analyzed for their curative as well as their destructive processes. Much of the recent advances in understanding the structure of DNA and the complex proteins was brought about by analyses carried out by biophysicists. Sporting equipment companies and athletic coaches are now relying on information from biophysicists for the design of their products and for new techniques in training athletes.

Thermophysicists study how heat can be changed into work, how it is produced, how it is transferred from one place to another, and how it changes matter. Heat energy pushes the pistons of engines and turns the blades of turbines. It can easily be turned into electrical or mechanical energy. Over one-third of the fuel in today's automobile engines is wasted as heat energy instead of being efficiently converted to mechanical power. Thermophysicists are looking for ways to produce engines that will run cooler and provide more horsepower for the fuel they burn. The microwave oven is a new tool invented by physicists that flip-flops the molecules in foods, cooking them faster and with less energy than with ordinary electric stoves.

Electricity and magnetism are closely related. Electricity can produce magnetism, and magnetism can produce electricity. Physicists who unraveled this important relationship led man to the modern age. Huge generators provide the electric current that runs the labor-saving devices in our homes and the powerful machines in industry. Electricity provides light, heat, and air conditioning. Physicists are constantly working at improvements and innovations in the field of electromagnetism.

Electronics is the branch of physics that studies the behavior of electrons, especially in vacuum- or gas-filled tubes and in special materials

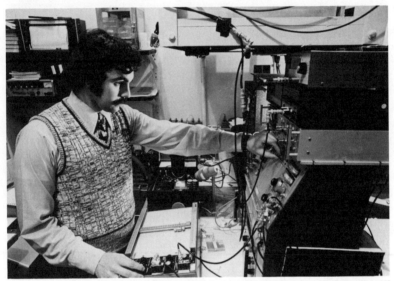

BELL LABS

In experimentation on semiconductors, a scientist measures the feedback profile of dopant distribution in gallium arsenide samples.

known as semiconductors. Electronics has made possible most of the modern wonders of communication including radio, television, and the telephone. It has resulted in the development of radar, automobile ignition systems, and the computer.

Other physicists are involved in physics education or are interested in the history and philosophy of this ancient science. Many people trained in physics deal with the administrative details of funding and managing ongoing research and development projects. Many also work at industrial facilities implementing new physics discoveries into practical products that improve our way of living.

Where Are Physicists Employed?

About 48,000 people worked as physicists in 1976. By 1985, the Federal government predicts, there will be a need for about 60,000 trained physicists. Nearly one-third of these will be employed by private industry. The largest industrial employers are the electronic and computing equipment companies and the electrical machinery manufacturers. These are followed by companies that produce other machinery, the aircraft and aerospace industries, transportation and automobile manufacturers, and defense-related concerns.

About 40 percent of all physicists worked for colleges or universities, where they taught and carried out research. Many others worked in hospitals, commercial research laboratories, and for the military. About 5,000 physicists were employed by the Federal government in 1978, mostly in the Departments of Defense and Commerce.

Although physicists are employed in all parts of the country, their employment is greatest in areas that have heavy industrial concentrations and where there are large universities. Nearly one-fourth of all physicists work in four metropolitan areas—Washington, DC, Boston, New York City, and Los Angeles. In fact, over one-third of all physicists live in California, New York, or Massachusetts.

How Can I Become a Physicist?

Most entry-level jobs in physics require some graduate training beyond the bachelor's degree. The Ph.D. degree is required for almost all faculty jobs at colleges and universities, and for many research positions. However, there are openings for those with bachelor's or master's degrees.

Those having bachelor's degrees qualify for some applied research and development jobs in private industry and in the Federal government. They work on implementing the theoretical aspects of physics into everyday applications. With a bachelor's degree in physics and some course credit in education, a person can often find work as a teacher in a secondary school system or at many community colleges. Some people who find work as laboratory technologists in physics, work alongside physicists and engineers engaged in advanced research. These technologists often continue their education on a part-time basis, and many eventually receive advanced degrees that allow them to assume more responsible positions. Many with a bachelor's degree in physics do not become physicists, but apply their physics training to jobs in engineering, medicine, computer programming, and other scientific fields.

With a doctorate in physics you are prepared for a research career, and you may have to assume the responsibility for major projects that involve many people and cost hundreds of thousands of dollars. At an industrial laboratory the research usually involves the application of basic theoretical concepts. Physicists in industrial labs are involved in such projects as solar cell technology, data communications, petroleum product processing, the design of advanced computer circuitry, and the growing of new superconducting crystals.

Research at a government laboratory or a nonprofit research center involves defense applications, consumer protection, weather prediction, the maintenance of industrial standards, the development of new industrial techniques, geophysical studies, and also some basic research.

Most basic research, however, is carried out at colleges and universities, where federally and privately financed inquiries into the nature of the universe take place. At these institutions, many of this country's brightest physicists work with their graduate students on projects that are not necessarily concerned with direct product application. College and university faculty, all with doctorates and most with postdoctoral training, divide their time between teaching and research. Their research may involve billion-dollar particle accelerators that literally smash atoms to reveal subatomic particles, or they may engage in studying how materials behave when cooled within a millionth of a degree of absolute zero, or they may be interested in how a prick of a person's finger is registered as pain by the brain.

Students planning a career in physics should have an inquisitive mind, high mathematical ability, and imagination. They should be able to work on their own, since physicists, particularly in basic research, often receive only limited supervision. And they should be able to work as part of a research team with scientists from other disciplines.

Physicists often begin their careers doing routine laboratory tasks. After some experience, they are assigned more complex tasks and may advance to work as project leaders or research directors. Some advance to top management jobs where they direct government research agencies or multinational corporations. Physicists who develop new products frequently form their own companies or join new firms to exploit their original ideas.

Specialization in physics is usually for graduate students. If, for instance, you are interested in nuclear physics, you would first obtain a bachelor's degree in physics with advanced training in mathematics, and then you would study advanced nuclear physics topics as you worked toward your master's and doctoral degrees. To become a physicist a typical candidate would have taken:

a) in high school—biology, chemistry, physics, advanced algebra, geometry, trigonometry, and, often, two years of a foreign language.

b) in the freshman and sophomore years of college—electricity and magnetism, classical mechanics, dynamics of particles and motion,

contemporary and nuclear topics, calculus, chemistry, English, foreign language, and general education courses such as psychology, economics, and history.
c) in the junior and senior years—wave and quantum physics, electronics, electromagnetic theory, relativity, statistical mechanics, differential equations, matrix algebra, and computer science.

In graduate school, the physics major takes specific courses in the area of specialization as well as advanced computer and mathematics instruction. The student will also begin a physics research project under the supervision of the graduate faculty, which will culminate in a Ph.D. dissertation. Even after the doctorate is received, many physicists then spend one or two years as low-paid postdoctoral students learning advanced techniques at a major university under the supervision of a prominent physicist.

Almost one-third of the people who receive bachelor's degrees in physics go to graduate work in another field. About one-half of those who do not go immediately to graduate school, but who seek employment after receiving their B.S. degree, find work in a field that does not make extensive use of their physics training. Since a bachelor's degree in physics provides a broad scientific background and the development of a keen mind that enjoys analytical research, the physics major is excellent preparation for many job opportunities. Physics training is directly applicable in computer science and engineering; it is also valuable in applying to medical school, law school, and to the industrial business world.

What Are My Chances of Getting a Job as a Physicist?

Employment opportunities in physics are expected to be favorable through the mid-1980's. Increasing interest in energy conservation and the production of nonfossil fuel power should encourage government- and industry-financed research and development in physics. There should be more than 1,100 openings each year for physicists.

Current Federal predictions, based on declining jobs in the 1970's, indicate that competition for doctoral-level positions will be keen. However, the number of graduate degrees awarded annually in physics has also been declining. Academic jobs may be hard to find, but many industrial and nonuniversity faculty positions are requiring the doctorate for entry-level jobs.

At the bachelor's and master's level, the employment prospects in physics are at least as good as those in other sciences and in most engineering disciplines. Some new graduates will find employment as engineers, technicians, and in the computer sciences. Others will find opportunities as high school physics teachers after completing the required educational courses and obtaining a state teaching certificate.

Physics, like all the physical sciences, is primarily the reserve of white men. Only about 3 percent of physicists are female, and about 3 percent are black. However, the situation is improving. Federal pressures as well as an awareness of the capabilities of women and minorities are causing an increase in the hiring of these groups. Improved enrollments in undergraduate and graduate physics programs by women and nonwhites will allow for greater participation in the field.

How Much Do Physicists Earn?

Physicists have relatively high salaries. Starting salaries for physicists with a bachelor's degree averaged around $14,000 a year in 1978. Those with a master's degree could expect to start at an average salary of $17,400, and those with a Ph.D. averaged $24,000.

The average salary for experienced physicists in 1978 was over $29,000. The 4,835 male physicists employed by the Federal government had an average salary of $31,521 in 1978, and the average salary of the 134 female physicists was $25,603.

In 1978 starting salaries on college and university faculties for physics professors with a Ph.D. was around $17,000. A full professor of physics at a major university earned about $26,500 in 1978. Many physics faculty, however, supplement their income by working as consultants and taking on special research projects.

Where Can I Obtain Training in Physics?

Some of the colleges and universities that offer a major in physics are:

Adelphi University, Garden City, Long Island, New York 11530
University of Arizona, Tucson, Arizona 85721
Brooklyn College, Brooklyn, New York 11210
Bucknell University, Lewisburg, Pennsylvania 17837
California Institute of Technology, Pasadena, California 91109
University of California, Berkeley, California 94720, Los Angeles, California 90024, Santa Barbara, California 93106
California State University, Fullerton, California 92634
Case Western Reserve University, Cleveland, Ohio 44106
University of Colorado, Boulder, Colorado 80302
Cooper Union, New York, N.Y. 10003
Cornell University, Ithaca, New York 14850
Drexel University, Philadelphia, Pennsylvania 19104
Fairleigh Dickinson University, Rutherford, New Jersey 07070
Georgia Institute of Technology, Atlanta, Georgia 30332
Harvard University, Cambridge, Massachusetts 02138
Harvey Mudd College, Claremont, California 91711

University of Illinois, Urbana, Illinois 61801
Iowa State University, Ames, Iowa 50010
Louisiana State University, Baton Rouge, Louisiana 70803
Manhattan College, New York, N.Y. 10471
University of Maryland, College Park, Maryland 20742
Massachusetts Institute of Technology, Cambridge, Massachusetts 02139
Miami University, Oxford, Ohio 45056
University of Michigan, Ann Arbor, Michigan 48104
Michigan State University, East Lansing, Michigan 48824
University of Minnesota, Minneapolis, Minnesota 55455
New Mexico State University, Las Cruces, New Mexico 88003
New York University, New York, N.Y. 10003
Oberlin College, Oberlin, Ohio 44074
Ohio State University, Columbus, Ohio 43212
Pennsylvania State University, University Park, Pennsylvania 16802
Purdue University, West Lafayette, Indiana 47907
Rensselaer Polytechnic Institute, Troy, New York 12181
Rice University, Houston, Texas 77001
Rutgers University, New Brunswick, New Jersey 08903
State University, of New York, Stony Brook, New York 11790
Tufts University, Medford, Massachusetts 02155
U.S. Air Force Academy, U.S.A.F.A., Colorado 80840
U.S. Naval Academy, Annapolis, Maryland 21402
Virginia Polytechnical Institute, Blacksburg, Virginia 24061
University of Wisconsin, Madison, Wisconsin 53706
Yale University, New Haven, Connecticut 06520

Where Can I Get More Information About Physics?

The American Institute of Physics has a number of member societies that can help you in selecting a career.

The American Physical Society has as its objective the advancement and diffusion of the knowledge of physics. All branches of fundamental and applied physics are generally included in its scope. Both experimental and theoretical researches are reported in its journals and meetings.

The Optical Society of America devotes itself to the advancement of optics, pure and applied, in all its branches. Its scope includes research in fundamental optics as well as problems concerned with design and production of optical instruments.

The Acoustical Society of America has as its purpose to increase and diffuse the knowledge of acoustics and promote its practical applications. The scope includes architectural acoustics, engineering acoustics, noise, psychological and physiological acoustics, shock and vibration, speech communication, underwater acoustics, physical acoustics, and musical acoustics.

The Society of Rheology is composed of physicists, chemists, and engineers interested in rheology, which is defined as the science of deformation and flow of matter. Rheology includes both phenomenological and molecular theories, instrumentation, and the study of materials such as plastics, metals, ceramics, rubbers, paint, glass, and foodstuffs.

The American Association of Physics Teachers provides a much needed forum for the discussion of the problems of teaching. In cooperation with other groups, it promotes the advancement of physics and emphasizes its place in the general culture.

The American Crystallographic Association has as its objective the promotion of the study of the arrangement of the atoms in matter, its causes, its nature, and its consequences, and of the tools and methods used in such studies.

The American Astronomical Society has as its purpose the advancement of astronomy and closely related branches of science.

The American Association of Physicists in Medicine has as its purposes to promote the application of physics to medicine and biology, to encourage interest and training in medical physics and related fields, and to disseminate technical information in medical physics.

The American Vacuum Society has as its purpose the advancement and diffusion of the knowledge of vacuum science, both fundamental and applied. Its scope includes all areas of science and technology wherein pressures below atmospheric are essential.

Write to them at:

The American Institute of Physics
335 East 45th Street
New York, NY 10017

They also have a student program, called the Society of Physics Students, which you may be interested in joining.

For information concerning Federal employment write to:

Interagency Board of U.S. Civil Service
1900 E Street, N.W.
Washington, DC 20415

For detailed information about careers in physics, read:

Your Future in Physics by Raymond M. Bell. Richards Rosen Press, Inc.
Your Future in Nuclear Energy Fields by W. E. Thomson. Richards Rosen Press, Inc.

Chapter VII

The Life Sciences: The Biological Sciences, Biochemistry

LIFE SCIENCES

Life scientists study the nature, structure, function, and behavior of living things. They are concerned not only with the myriad forms of life but also with evolution, the physical, social, and psychological development of organisms, and the relationships between living things and the environment. Biology is too broad a science for any single person to comprehend or to investigate; therefore, life scientists specialize in one of the many branches of the science.

The biological sciences may be subdivided in various ways. The two major categories are *botany,* the study of plants, and *zoology,* the study of animals. Within each of these large categories are numerous smaller branches.

What Are the Branches of the Life Sciences?

All of the many fields of the life sciences are related to each other in some way. The traditional delineations of even botany and zoology cannot stay distinct, since a scientist studying even one specific organism must encompass in his research the habitat, evolution, structure, chemistry, weather conditions, predators, food, and so forth with which the life form coexists.

Let us look at the main subdivisions of the life sciences, and within each we can discuss some of the occupations involved.

1. *Botanists* study plants and their environments. Few botanists study all aspects of plant life. Most work in specific areas of research. *Plant anatomists* are interested in the structural parts of plants. They are concerned with the roots, the stems, and the leaves. Botanists want to know how the plant makes its food. *Plant biochemists* study the photosynthetic reaction. Others are interested in the nongreen plants, which cannot directly convert sunlight into food.

There are life scientists who want to discover the mechanisms by which water and minerals are circulated throughout the plant. *Plant*

68

geneticists are studying the ways in which plants reproduce. They want to know the interrelationships between the fruit, the seed, and the flower. They strive to make sturdier, healthier plants.

Many botanists specialize in one class of plants. *Mycologists* study fungi. *Lichenologists* study lichens. *Phycologists* are interested in algae.

Agronomists are life scientists who work with farmers. They are sometimes called agricultural scientists. They are concerned with developing and improving the quality of crops, such as corn, wheat, and cotton. They try to find better ways for planting, growing, and harvesting grains, fruits, and vegetables. They work with agricultural chemists to produce fertilizers. Often, through research with geneticists, new breeds of crops can be developed that are healthier and more resistant to disease and insect infestation. New crops can also be designed to grow faster or with special properties that will make them more desirable to farmers, wholesalers, and consumers.

Plant pathologists (phytopathology) study diseases in plants and work with plant physiologists and biochemists in developing cures. Crop production is also dependent on an understanding of the soil, so agronomists work with soil scientists to determine ways of increasing acreage yields and decreasing soil erosion.

Horticulturists work with orchard and garden plants such as fruit and nut trees, vegetables, and flowers. They try to improve the various varieties. Horticulturists are involved in the beautification of communities, homes, parks, and other areas as well as in increasing crop quality and yields.

2. *Zoologists* study various aspects of animal life—its origins, behavior, and life processes. Some zoologists study live animals in laboratory, zoological park, or natural surroundings. Others dissect animals to study the structure of their parts.

Many fields of zoology are identified by the animal groups studied. *Mammalogists* study mammals, *ornithologists* study birds, *herpetologists* study reptiles and amphibians, *ichthyologists* are interested in fish, *entomologists* study insects, *helminthologists* study worms, and *protozoologists* investigate the lives and behavior of one-celled animals.

Animal husbandry specialists do research on the breeding, feeding, and diseases of farm animals. *Veterinarians* study diseases in animals and learn to treat their ailments and complaints.

3. One specialty among the life sciences is *anatomy*. *Anatomists* study the structure of living organisms. They analyze the composition of cells, tissues, and organ systems.

Gross anatomists specialize in large structures such as the organs in man. They analyze and study the heart, the lungs, the reproductive organs, the liver, and so on. *Comparative anatomists* compare the anatomies of different plants and animals to discover evolutionary trends and to try to understand the interrelationship of various natural functions.

Histology is the study of tissues, groups of similar cells that perform a specific function for the organism. *Serologists* study blood tissue, *dermatologists* study skin tissue, *osteologists* study bones, *myologists* study muscles, and *neurologists* investigate nerves.

Cytology is the study of cells. *Cytologists* use high-powered optical microscopes and electron microscopes to study the life processes occurring at the cellular level. They have developed microsurgical techniques to remove the nucleus from a living cell. *Enzymologists* study how enzymes, which are biological catalysts, function within organisms.

4. Some life scientists are interested in learning how nature passes on information from one generation to the next. *Geneticists* study the transmission and function of hereditary material, such as chromosomes, genes, and DNA. *Embryologists* are interested in the formation and development of living animals from a fertilized egg through the hatching period or through gestation. They investigate the causes of healthy and abnormal development in animals.

5. The smallest living organisms are an important concern of life scientists, since many affect our health and our environment. *Microbiology* is the general name for life scientists who study microscopic plants and animals. In a drop of water from a pond, you can find many life forms. Some are one-celled creatures such as the amoeba and the paramecium; others are multicelled, like the hydra whose tentacles wave even smaller organisms toward its primitive mouth. The euglena is a one-celled link between plants and animals, which can swim freely, but still manufactures food within its chloroplasts.

Bacteriologists study the small, nongreen bacteria plants. Some bacteria are beneficial to man; our digestion is aided by bacteria in the intestine. Others cause disease. Some bacteria help break down dead material so that the nitrogen and other chemicals can return to the soil, and some pollute our streams so that they become nonpotable.

Virologists study viruses, which are at the very threshold of life. Viruses usually consist of only a thread of DNA surrounded by a protein coating. Since viruses do not possess the necessary cell parts for reproduction and other life processes, they must invade living cells and utilize the host's cellular machinery. Viruses are the causes of many of mankind's worst diseases, such as polio, and many virologists are investigating a viral link to cancer.

6. *Pathology* is the study of disease. *Pathologists* specialize in effects of diseases, parasites, and insects on human and animal cells, tissues, and organs. Some pathologists investigate genetic variations caused by drugs. *Phytopathologists* study the diseases among plants.

Immunologists study the microorganisms and other substances that provide immunity from disease. They work with medical microbiologists in investigating antibiotic responses and other ways in which the body fights infections.

Parasitologists investigate parasites such as hookworm, which can cause disease. In Africa, several kinds of parasite infect the land, killing men, cattle, and crops. *Epidemiologists* are life scientists who study epidemic diseases that can sicken and kill millions of people. There is even a field called *gnotobiotics,* in which life scientists study the effects of a germ-free environment on living species. Hundreds of small animals have been raised under these conditions and have led disease-free lives. Some humans have depressed immunological responses in their bodies and can die if infected by even a cold virus. A Texas boy who suffers from this condition spends his life in a germ-free room. He eats only specially cooked foods in which all bacteria have been killed. *Gnotobiologists* are helping him survive.

7. *Ecologists* study the relationship between organisms and their environments. They investigate how such environmental influences as rainfall, temperature, pollutants, and other forms of animal and plant life affect organisms. Ecologists may examine samples of plankton, microscopic plants and animals, from the sea to determine the effects on ocean life of oil spills from tankers. They may go to the tops of mountains to count eagle chicks whose shells were affected by DDT. Some urban ecologists constantly monitor the water and air in our cities for various pollutants.

Biosociologists study how groups of living things get along together. They are interested in schools of fish, gaggles of geese, herds of elephants, and so forth. They are also interested in the interrelationships between several species that might share a meadow or a watering hole.

Biogeographers study the geographical distribution of living things. Similar plants and animals in Africa and South America suggest that once a giant continent separated, splitting into our modern land forms. *Phytogeographers* specialize in plants and the land forms where they exist, and *zoogeographers* specialize in animal forms at different geologic locations.

Biological limnologists study living things in rivers and lakes. *Marine biologists* are concerned with living species in the oceans. *Biometeorologists* are concerned with those in the atmosphere, such as airborne bacteria. And *exobiologists* are studying living things in space and on other planets.

8. *Paleontologists* are life scientists who are interested in life that existed on the earth before modern man. They study fossils that are discovered in the earth's crust. They have been able to reconstruct animal and plant life that has disappeared. From their researches, we have learned about dinosaurs that once roamed New Jersey, saber-toothed tigers in California, and a huge sea that covered the Midwest. *Anthropologists* are life scientists who specialize in studying the fossil remains of man and his early ancestors.

9. The life sciences, of course, necessitate an understanding of many other scientific disciplines. Some occupations, however, especially interrelate two or more disciplines. Human engineers study living man as

a machine. Electronics specialists and physicians working with these human engineers have developed the field of *bionics*. Bionics has produced prosthetic devices and synthetic organs to assist the disabled and to prolong the lives of the seriously ill. *Cybernetics* is the use of biology, mathematics, and psychology in the study of the relationship between living things and complex mechanical devices, such as computers. Through cybernetics, scientists hope to design machines that can better serve mankind.

10. *Biochemistry* involves the use of chemistry in the study of living things. *Biochemists* study the chemical composition and behavior of organisms. Life is, simply, a product of complex chemical combinations and reactions. Therefore, to understand how nature works, biochemists investigate the chemistry of reproduction, growth, heredity, respiration, and so on.

Photosynthesis, for example, is the chemical combination of water and carbon dioxide, in the presence of light, to make sugar. The reactants and the products have been known for over two hundred years; however, the mechanism, or means, by which the reaction takes place is still not completely understood. There is now strong evidence to suggest that the light reaction of photosynthesis involves two simultaneous systems. One involves chlorophyll a-type molecules and a very strong electron acceptor, called ferredoxin, which passes the energy to nicotine amide dinucleotide phosphate. The second stage involves chlorophyll b-type molecules, carotenes, and plastoquinones. As you can see, biochemistry is far more complicated than the simplistic reactions outlined in your high school textbooks.

The methods and techniques of biochemistry are applied in medicine, nutrition, and agriculture. Biochemists may investigate the causes and cures for diseases, identify the nutrients necessary to maintain good health, or develop chemical compounds for pest control.

Some specialties related closely to biochemistry are *nutrition* and *pharmacology*. *Nutritionists* examine the bodily processes through which food is utilized and transformed into energy. They learn how vitamins, minerals, proteins, and other nutrients build and repair tissues. They are concerned with developing diets for ill patients, as well as advising healthy people on what to eat in order to maintain their well-being.

Pharmacologists develop and test new drugs. They use animals such as rats, guinea pigs, and monkeys to determine the effects of new products. Long before a drug is marketed, the pharmacologist must prove that it is not harmful and that it is effective in treating the disorder. They also test the effects of gases, poisons, pollutants, cigarettes, and other substances on the functioning of organs and tissues.

11. In the past, most food preparation was carried out in the home. People would either eat freshly prepared produce or store it in cellars. The stored foods were pickled, smoked, or salted. Today, however, almost all foods are processed in industry. A key worker involved in

seeing that you have safe foods is the *food scientist* or *food technologist*. Food scientists apply their knowledge of chemistry, biology, and physics to the processing, preserving, packaging, distributing, and storing of food. About three-fifths of all food scientists work in developing new techniques for handling food. They research new sources for protein; examine the factors that affect the flavor, texture, or appearance of foods; and study the effects of microorganisms in the decay of products. Many food technologists work in quality assurance laboratories, periodically examining and inspecting food products.

12. Other life scientists are involved in biological education. They teach in high schools, community colleges, colleges, and universities. Some life scientists are interested in the history and philosophy of biology and medicine. Many life scientists handle the administrative details of funding and managing research projects. Others work at hospitals and at public health facilities. Some are salespeople for pharmaceutical houses or work in agribusiness, the large industrialized food growing, processing, and sales companies.

Where Are Life Scientists Employed?

There were about 225,000 persons working as life scientists in 1978. About one-third are involved in work dealing with food and agriculture, about one-half work as biologists, and the rest are involved in biochemistry and medical science research.

Colleges and universities employ nearly three-fifths of all life scientists, in both teaching and research jobs. Medical schools and hospitals employ large numbers of life scientists.

Sizeable numbers of biologists work for state agricultural departments, which are usually associated with colleges and agricultural experiment stations. At these bureaus, agronomists improve crops, horticulturalists develop techniques for growing fruits and new species of flowers, veterinary scientists work on cures for animal diseases, entomologists study how bees cultivate orchards, and much vital farm research is carried out.

Food scientists in Idaho work with potato growers, as well as with frozen food processors and potato chip manufacturers. In Michigan they work with cereal manufacturers. Food chemists have found ways of rapidly ripening tomatoes so that they can be picked prematurely in Florida and under their supervision sprayed with ethylene glycol before being shipped North.

About 30,000 life scientists worked for the Federal government in 1978. Over half worked for the Department of Agriculture, which has research and aide stations throughout the U.S. A large agricultural station is in Beltsville, Maryland, where turkeys have been bred with overdeveloped breasts, since most Americans prefer white meat. Large numbers of life scientists work for the Department of the Interior and in the National Institutes of Health. One group at the Department of the Treasury examines alcohol and cigarette products for taxation violations. Another team at the Department of Commerce checks fibers for the textile industry. At the National Institutes of Health, government-financed disease research is being carried out by the leading life scientists of our country. At this huge research facility, in Bethesda, Maryland, intensive studies are being carried out on cancer, heart disease, mental disorders, birth defects, and many other serious ailments that require expensive, intensive research.

State and local governments employed about 30,000 life scientists. In addition to those working on agricultural products, many work for public health departments and environmental protection agencies, where they inspect restaurants and groceries, food-processing plants, and water and sewage facilities and check the air, the rivers, and so on. Nutritionists work for schools and hospitals, insuring that proper foods are served.

Approximately 50,000 life scientists worked in private industry. Most of them worked for companies that manufactured drugs, insecticides, or cosmetics, or they worked in the food industry. Some develop products in a research laboratory, and others do quality checks off an assembly line.

Biological laboratory research involves weighing, filtering, distilling, drying, and culturing (growing microorganisms). Precision and patience are of the utmost importance in laboratory science. Biological research often calls for working with animals. Sometimes the animal must be sacrificed, and often it is subjected to harsh treatment so that we can learn about nature and find ways to help humans suffering from terrible diseases. No biologist should be too squeamish about blood or about dissecting animals; that is how science progresses.

Biologists use a variety of tools and instruments, including electron microscopes, ultracentrifuges, nuclear magnetic spectrographs, optical microscopes, and automated sampling devices. Some experiments may call for radioactive tracers. Computer knowledge is becoming more and more essential for work in the life sciences.

The results of the work of life scientists may be published in scientific journals, harvested in Japan, slaughtered at a packing house in Chicago, injected in a patient in a leukemia ward, or given to a loved one as a present.

Life scientists are distributed fairly evenly throughout the U.S. It is one of the few scientific occupations in which you can live and work in rural communities. However, a large number of jobs are still concentrated in the major metropolitan areas where the universities and hospitals are located. Curiously enough, over 6 percent of all agricultural and biological scientists work in the Washington, D.C., area. If you want to teach in the life sciences above the community college or high school level, then, too, you will have to settle near a large city.

How Can I Become a Life Scientist?

A few opportunities exist for high school graduates in the life sciences as assistants and helpers. However, most technician-level jobs require at least two years of college plus on-the-job training, and some require a minimum of a bachelor's degree in biology or a related field.

The U.S. Department of Labor suggests that anyone seeking a career in the life sciences should plan to obtain an advanced degree.

The bachelor's degree is the usual minimum requirement for interesting work in industry or for the Federal government. A life scientist at this level can carry out the research proposed by project leaders or can perform tests, such as examining foods for microorganisms. Promotions, however, usually go to those with higher degrees. Biological sales and service technician jobs can usually be had with a bachelor's degree. Many life scientists begin their careers at the bachelor's level and continue to study toward a master's degree or a Ph.D. Often this on-the-job training is paid for by the employer.

A master's degree is generally required for any employment that requires independent work, and a doctorate is becoming the minimum degree for research work and university teaching. Most undergraduate and high school teaching jobs also require at least a master's.

High school students who want to prepare for a career in the life sciences should make sure that they have a good foundation in the basic skills before beginning college. English is important, since the written and spoken word is the means by which biologists communicate. The studying of a science requires careful textbook and journal reading, as well as good skills in compositional writing. Research papers and speeches at conferences are the principal means by which scientists learn of each other's work, which is vital for improving their own research.

Computer science and mathematics are essential in today's life science work. Algebra, geometry, trigonometry, and, especially, statistics are the tools that biologists use in analyzing their work. Foreign languages are important for communicating with scientists in other countries and for reading scientific works that are not translated into English.

The social studies courses help you understand the interrelationships between technology, science, economics, and the historical development of mankind.

In high school you should take every science course that is available. Biology, chemistry, and physics are fundamental to your understanding of how living systems operate. If you can also take an ecology or oceanography course, you will find these very useful.

Art and photography are used by biologists to illustrate their research and to record their observations. If you are skilled and trained in these fields, you will have a distinct advantage in the life sciences.

Students planning a career in the life sciences should be able to work independently and as part of a team. They must have a great deal of patience and perseverance, since the work may often be tedious and repetitive. Also, they must not be easily frustrated, since research often leads to "blind alleys" or to inconclusive results. The field may require physical stamina and the ability to endure discomfort.

The first two years of college training in the life sciences generally consist of courses in general universal biology, anatomy and physiology, and, often, molecular biology or biochemistry. This is accompanied by work in general chemistry, qualitative analysis, organic chemistry, and calculus.

The junior and senior year college courses are often in the specialized life sciences. During this period, the student may study horticulture, agronomy, taxonomy, genetics, physiology, and so forth.

. In graduate school the life science major will receive advanced training in his or her area of interest. At the doctoral level, the student writes a dissertation based on original research carried out under the supervision of an expert.

In the life sciences there has been a rapid rise in the number of bachelor's and master's degrees awarded each year. The number of doctorates given, however, peaked in 1973 and is continuing to fall off. Women earned almost a fourth of the bioscience doctorates during the 1970's and are finding many exciting jobs in their fields.

What Are My Chances for Getting a Job as a Life Scientist?

It should not be too difficult to obtain a job as a life scientist if you have an advanced degree. There should be about 12,000 openings a year.

Employment will increase as a result of more interest in medical research and concern about the environment. As new laws and standards regarding environmental safeguards and testing are passed by legislatures, industry will be required to hire more life scientists. The government, too, will need more skilled technologists to inspect and test the products and wastes given off by factories and industrial plants.

More government and private spending on cancer and medical research is expected in the 1980's. This will create new jobs for microbiologists, biochemists, virologists, laboratory animal keepers, pharmacologists, and so on.

The development of synthetic fuel substitutes, too, will create jobs for biologists, who will have to test the safety of the emissions. Alcohol produced from grain is being considered as a renewable fuel resource. Also, cottonwood-type trees, which grow rapidly, may be used as a heating fuel. Agricultural scientists will be needed to develop better harvesting and processing methods for these crops.

A life science degree is useful, too, for entry to occupations related to biology, such as medical laboratory technology, medical salesman, or any other health-care occupation.

Employment in the life sciences is expected to increase faster than the average for all occupations during the 1980's.

How Much Do Life Scientists Earn?

Life scientists receive relatively high salaries. In the Federal government in 1978, life scientists with a bachelor's degree could begin at over $11,000 a year. With a master's, the starting salary was as high as $20,000, and with a Ph.D., a biologist could start at over $24,000.

In private industry salaries are usually not as high, except for those with specialized training. Food scientists with a bachelor's degree started in 1977 with salaries over $11,300; with a master's, they could start at $13,500; and with a Ph.D., the starting salary was $17,400. Experienced biochemists in industry averaged $18,000 for those with a bachelor's degree, $19,000 for those with a master's, and $26,000 for those with a doctorate.

Earnings of experienced life scientists averaged about $25,000 in 1978. This was more than twice the average income of nonsupervisory workers in this country for that year.

The average salary for a full professor in the life sciences at a university was $26,470 in 1978. For assistant professors the starting salary averaged around $17,000; however, a Ph.D. is required by almost all teaching institutions today.

Most life scientists work in well-lighted, well-ventilated, clean laboratories. They usually work 5-day, 35-hour workweeks and have liberal hospital and fringe benefits. Some jobs, however, require strenuous work outdoors under extreme conditions. Other jobs may require arduous around-the-clock data gathering. These jobs are very exciting for the scientists who choose them, and, often, the thrill of creative research is the greatest reward of all.

Where Can I Obtain Training in the Life Sciences?

Some of the colleges and universities that offer a major in the biological sciences are:

Adrian College, Adrian, Michigan 49221
Albion College, Albion, Michigan 49224
Albright College, Reading, Pennsylvania 19604
Allegheny College, Meadville, Pennsylvania 16335
Antioch College, Yellow Springs, Ohio 45387
Bates College, Lewiston, Maine 04240
Bethany College, Bethany, West Virginia 26032
Boston College, Chestnut Hill, Massachusetts 02167
Bowdoin College, Brunswick, Maine 04011

Brandeis University, Waltham, Massachusetts 02154
Brown University, Providence, Rhode Island 02912
Capital University, Columbus, Ohio 43209
Carleton College, Northfield, Minnesota 55057
Central Missouri State University, Warrensburg, Missouri 64093
University of Chicago, Chicago, Illinois 60637
Clark University, Worcester, Massachusetts 01610
Clemson University, Clemson, South Carolina 29631
University of Dayton, Dayton, Ohio 45469
University of Delaware, Newark, Delaware 19711
Earlham College, Richmond, Indiana 47374
East Texas State University, Commerce, Texas 75428
Eastern Michigan University, Ypsilanti, Michigan 48197
University of Evansville, Evansville, Indiana 47702
Florence State University, Florence, Alabama 35630
Fordham University, New York, N.Y. 10021
Furman University, Greenville, South Carolina 29613
Georgetown University, Washington, D.C. 20007
Gettysburg College, Gettysburg, Pennsylvania 17325
Hamilton College, Clinton, New York 13323
Hampton Institute, Hampton, Virginia 23368
Hobart and William Smith College, Geneva, New York 14456
Hofstra University, Hempstead, New York 11550
Kalamazoo College, Kalamazoo, Michigan 49001
Kenyon College, Gambler, Ohio 43022
Lafayette College, Easton, Pennsylvania 18042
Lehigh University, Bethlehem, Pennsylvania 18015
Lycoming College, Williamsport, Pennsylvania 17701
Madison College, Harrisonburg, Virginia 22801
Marietta College, Marietta, Ohio 45750
Marquette University, Milwaukee, Wisconsin 53233
Miami University, Oxford, Ohio 45056
Muhlenberg College, Allentown, Pennsylvania 18104
New York University, New York, N.Y. 10003
Northeastern University, Boston, Massachusetts 02115
Oberlin College, Oberlin, Ohio 44074
Occidental College, Los Angeles, California 90041
University of Rochester, Rochester, New York 14627
Siena College, Loudonville, New York 12211
Stanford University, Stanford, California 94305
State University of New York, Albany, Binghamton, and Buffalo, New
     York
Trinity College, Hartford, Connecticut 06106
Tufts University, Medford, Massachusetts 02155
Vanderbilt University, Nashville, Tennessee 37240
Villanova University, Villanova, Pennsylvania 19085
University of Washington, Seattle, Washington 98195
Wayne State University, Detroit, Michigan 48202

West Virginia University, Morgantown, West Virginia 26506
Western Kentucky University, Bowling Green, Kentucky 42101
College of Wooster, Wooster, Ohio 44691

Where Can I Get More Information About the Life Sciences?

For further information on careers in the biological sciences write
to the following professional organizations:

American Institute of Biological Sciences
3900 Wisconsin Avenue N.W.
Washington, DC 20016

American Physiological Society
9650 Rockville Pike
Bethesda, MD 20014

Institute of Food Technology
Suite 2120; 221 North LaSalle Street
Chicago, IL 60601

Federation of American Societies for Experimental Biology
9650 Rockville Pike
Bethesda, MD 20014

American Society of Agronomy
677 South Segoe Road
Madison, WI 53711

For information about careers for biologists and biochemists in the
Federal government, write to:

U.S. Civil Service Commission
1900 E Street N.W.
Washington, DC 20415

U.S. Department of Agriculture
Department of Personnel
Washington, DC 20250

For detailed information, read:

Your Future in Agribusiness by Chester S. Hutchinson. Richards Rosen
Press, Inc.

Chapter **VIII**

The Environmental Sciences: Geology, Geophysics, Meteorology, Oceanography

GEOLOGY

Geology is the study of the earth. Geologists try to understand how the earth was formed and how it changes. They study rocks, soils, mountains, rivers, oceans, caves, glaciers, and other parts of the earth.

The earth was formed more than 4½ billion years ago. It has changed in many ways since then. Many of the changes occur slowly and will continue as long as the planet exists. Diastrophism is the geologic term that covers all the various forces that have caused the earth's crust to be deformed, producing continents, mountains, valleys, chasms, and so on. Earthquakes and volcanic eruptions have changed huge pieces of land, forming mountains out of deserts and causing islands to surface above the sea. Erosion from wind and rain has flattened craggy peaks into farmlands, and glaciers have carved U-shaped valleys through mountains of granite.

Water also changes the earth. Waves can wash away shorelines in one area of the earth and deposit new land in other regions. Rivers eat away mountains piece by piece, carrying the soil downriver to form enriched deltas, such as Mississippi and Egypt.

Some geologists study the remains of animals and plants that lived thousands of years ago. Their skeletons and imprints have become fossils, which tell us how life evolved on the earth.

Geology is usually subdivided into various fields of specialization, but each field is intimately related to the others. *Geophysics* is the study of earthquakes, the earth's magnetism, the heat flow within the earth, the earth's gravity, and the earth's interior. *Geochemistry* is the study of the chemical composition of the earth, its rocks and minerals. *Histori-*

cal geology is the study of the sequence of events that have occurred during the formation of the continents and oceans. *Mineralogy* is the study of the minerals of the earth's crust. *Petrology* is the study of the rocks of the earth's crust. *Structural geology* is the study of how the rocks and land formations were deformed and changed throughout the earth's history. *Stratigraphy* is the study of rocks formed from oceanic deposits, which can reveal the succession of biologic and geologic events. *Geomorphology* is the study of the earth's landforms. *Paleontology* is the study of fossils. *Paleoecology* is the study of ancient plant and animal communities. *Economic geology* is the study of ore-forming minerals and fuel deposits that can be mined or developed for industrial uses.

Some of the questions that geologists are trying to answer are:

What was the earth like twenty million years ago?
What kind of rock layers are capable of forming and holding oil deposits?
How was the Chesapeake Bay formed?
How can oilfields that contain only small amounts of fuel be productively utilized?
What was the driving force that separated the huge continental plates?
How were the craters of the moon formed?
What kinds of conditions within the earth produce from dead organic matter the wide range of carbon fuels: natural gas, crude oil, coal, and diamonds?

What Do Geologists Do?

Geologists study the earth's crust by examining rocks that they find on the surface and by drilling into the earth to recover rock cores. They identify rocks and minerals by testing them for hardness, density, color, microscopic details, and radioactivity and by analyzing them chemically.

Geologists use many tools and instruments such as hammers, chisels, levels, telescopes, electron and optical microscopes, gravity meters, cameras, compasses, and seismographs. They may analyze photomicrographs of a single rock, or they may examine river basin photographs taken from a satellite. The computer is becoming as important a tool for the geologist as it is for the other sciences.

Many geologists work in laboratories, where they carefully examine specimens found in the field by their associates. They test these specimens for physical and chemical properties. They may study fossil remains of animal and vegetable life. They might test the porosity of rocks by dripping oil or water through them. They may examine long core segments of an ocean bottom to determine what kind of life has swum in the ocean above over the last ten thousand years. Special equipment, such as the X-ray diffractometer, tells scientists how the molecules of a mineral crystallized.

Geologists are also called on to advise construction, environmental, and government agencies. They help plan the location of buildings, dams, and highways. Seemingly solid land may have a river flowing a few yards underneath or may be located near an earthquake fault. This information, when available, can save great expense and may avert disaster.

Some geologists administer and manage research and exploration work for the government or for mining or oil companies. Others may teach and work on research projects in colleges and universities.

Minerals are the pure compounds within and on the earth's surface. These are the source of the metals used by industry and society. *Mineralogists* are concerned with identifying and classifying all of the crystalline mineral compounds that are found at the earth's surface, within the earth's crust, in lunar and Martian materials, and in meteorites. Mineralogists determine the chemical elements that make up each mineral. They find the structural arrangement of the atoms within the crystal, using electron microscopes and X-ray spectrographs. They measure the physical properties of the mineral and try to discover the possible ways in which it may have been formed.

Petrologists study the composition, classification, and origin of rocks. Rocks are mixtures of many materials, including minerals, fossils, and others. If a rock was formed by cooling from molten, liquid earth, called magma, it is called an igneous rock. If it was formed at regular earth temperatures by the accumulation of mineral grains or by settling particles in lakes or the ocean, it is called a sedimentary rock. The third kind of rock is called metamorphic rock; these rocks were formed from sedimentary or igneous rocks that were subjected to heat and pressure sufficiently great that the crystal structure of the rock changed. Most petrologists specialize in either sedimentary, igneous, or metamorphic petrology. Ninety-five percent of the rocks on the earth's surface are sedimentary, and all of the oil and natural gas deposits are found in sedimentary rocks. Therefore *sedimentary petrology* is an excellent career. Igneous and metamorphic petrologists are concerned with rocks formed under high temperature or high pressure or both. Many of these rocks are deep within the earth. Petrologists use chemical analysis, X-ray crystallography, special petrographic microscopy, spectrographs, and, of course, the computer.

The *economic geologist* applies a broad knowledge of all branches of geology to the discovery, exploration, development, and exploitation of mineral deposits. This scientist works closely with other professionals such as the engineer, the physicist, the geophysicist, the geochemist, the statistician, and the economist to determine if and how a mineral

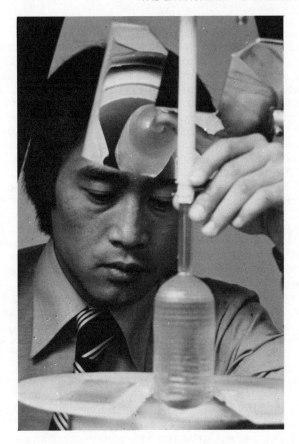

IBM

A researcher grows crystals in a furnace, observing them
through a specially designed mirror device.

or fuel discovery can be developed. For this career, sound business
principles is an essential requirement.

Paleontologists are concerned with collecting, preparing, studying,
and writing about fossils. Fossils include bones, teeth, shells, leaves,
pollen, fragments of animals and plants, imprints, tracks, burrows, and
coprolites (fossilized excrement). These biologist-geologists try to reconstruct the ancient environment and geography of the earth. Their finds
are the basis for our understanding of evolution. *Invertebrate paleontologists* study fossil animals without backbones, such as sponges, corals,
insects, and shellfish. *Vertebrate paleontologists* study fossil animals with

backbones, such as fish, amphibians, reptiles, birds, and mammals. *Paleobotanists* study fossilized plants.

The newest occupation in geology is *space geologist.* These scientists study the mineralogy, petrology, and geochemistry of rocks brought back by astronauts from the moon, examined by remote control on nearby planets, or that come to earth as meteorites. These extraterrestrial samples help us understand the origins of the solar system.

A *marine geologist* studies the geology of the ocean basins. These shipboard scientists describe, measure, and analyze the structures on and below the seafloor. Most specialize in particular areas such as deepwater environments, continental shelf environments, or coastal environments. Many rich oil fields have been found just off the continental shelfs of North America and northern Europe through studies by these experts. Rich mineral deposits and geothermal energy may be found under the oceans, which cover three-fourths of the planet's surface.

Geochemists study the earth and related planetary bodies from the standpoint of chemistry. They perform the analyses that determine the elements and compounds of rocks, minerals, and ores. Geochemists work with sensitive instruments to examine the finds sent to them by geologists in the field.

Geothermal geologists are interested in the heat within the earth, especially where it can be exploited by man. This heat generally occurs near or within igneous rocks. Sometimes water flows through these rocks, producing geysers and geothermal springs. Countries with geothermal resources, such as Iceland, have already tapped this "free" energy for heating and for production of electricity.

Geomorphologists are specially trained geologists who are interested in land formations, such as mountains, valleys, canyons, and plains. Geomorphology, which is closely associated with geography and topographic mapmaking, is becoming more important as the U.S. is becoming more aware of environmental factors in planning cities, recreation areas, and the exploitation of its mineral wealth. Geomorphologists determine how fresh water is distributed on and below the land surface, they study the effects of erosion on the land, and they are concerned with the regeneration of natural conditions after a mine or oil field runs out of its riches. Much geomorphology involves aerial photography and surveying skills, as well as the other tools of the geoscientist.

Petroleum geologists search for and recover oil and natural gas. Some petroleum geologists work near drilling sites; others, using computers, correlate petroleum-related geologic information for entire regions, so that new sites may be discovered. These scientists carefully study an area, noting its topography, its underlying rock structure, and other geophysical data. They set off explosions underground and record, with a seismograph, the kinds of vibrations sent through the earth. Sound travels faster through rock than through natural gas or oil pools. If they decide to drill an exploratory hole, then, in cooperation with *engi-*

neering geologists, they must determine the pressure, temperature, viscosity, and chemical composition of the material they hope to extract. Basic research is also being carried out by petroleum geologists with geochemists to try to understand how petroleum is produced by nature, how it can be recovered from oil shale, and how it might be manufactured synthetically.

Where Are Geologists Employed?

More than 34,000 people worked as geologists in 1976. More than 60 percent of them worked in private industry. Most geologists work for petroleum companies. Others work for mining and quarrying companies. Some are employed as consultants to construction firms that build roads, tunnels, and dams as well as housing and office developments.

Most geologists who work for petroleum companies are exploring for gas and oil. The majority are employed in the United States, but many work in other oil-producing areas such as Canada, Australia, the Middle East, and Indonesia. They do field mapping, make stratigraphic measurements, conduct seismic and gravimetric tests, and perform other geophysical studies. They also work in laboratories doing basic research.

Mining companies use geologists to determine the location and extent of ore reserves in established mining areas, as well as to locate new deposits. Many of these mines are in the Southwest of the United States, Alaska, and in other countries of the world such as South Africa, Brazil, and Chile.

Real-estate developers, banks, and investment firms employ geologists as consultants to help them evaluate properties. Railroads, chemical companies, ceramics firms, and utilities hire geologists to help them find new resources and to prepare for the future.

The Federal government employs over 2,500 geologists. Most work for the Department of the Interior at the U.S. Geological Survey. Others work for the Bureau of Reclamation, the Bureau of Mines, and the Federal Water Pollution Control Administration. The National Park Service also employs geologists. The Department of Agriculture, the National Oceanic and Atmospheric Administration, and the Army Corps of Engineers each have geologists who work with research teams in specialized areas. The National Aeronautics and Space Administration is the latest bureau of the Federal government to use the services of highly trained geologists.

State and local governments, too, employ geologists. About 2,000 work at local and regional geological survey departments and highway departments and participate in environmental planning.

Schools offer teaching jobs ranging from graduate-level faculty to junior high school earth science teacher. About 400 universities and colleges give degrees in one of the fields of geology, and at least 200 community colleges and 400 four-year colleges offer course work in geology. In all, these postsecondary schools employ over 4,000 persons to teach geology and related subjects. There are also about 16,000 secondary school teachers who are teaching courses in the earth sciences, although many cannot be considered geologists.

There are about 3,000 consulting geologists who are in business for themselves. They usually specialize in the geology of a particular area or have special skills, such as in the interpretation of aerial photographs, which makes them valuable for mineral or fuel resource exploration, to engineering concerns, or to industry.

Some geologists work for nonprofit research institutions, and others are employed by museums.

Employment of geologists is concentrated in those states with large mineral and oil deposits. Almost two-thirds of all geologists work in five states: Texas, California, Louisiana, Colorado, and Oklahoma. Some are employed by American firms overseas for varying periods of time.

How Can I Become a Geologist?

Most positions in the geological sciences require a minimum of a master's degree. Research jobs and university teaching require a Ph.D. Some jobs, particularly in the Federal government, can be found for geologists with a bachelor's degree, but these are becoming scarce. Therefore, you really need a strong academic interest if you want to become a geologist.

The education of a geologist depends on his or her area of specialization. A vertebrate paleontologist, for example, needs a strong background in zoology, comparative anatomy, and, in addition to general geology courses, coursework in paleontology. A petroleum geologist should have training in physical and inorganic chemistry, physics, engineering, and special courses in fluid dynamics, as well as his general geology work.

In high school, a future geologist should take as many mathematics and science courses as possible. Algebra, geometry, trigonometry, biology, chemistry, and physics are essential. Besides these, you can take earth science, astronomy, calculus, and advanced placement courses. If your school offers a course in computer programming, this would be a great help.

Take enough English so that you can express yourself clearly in writing and in speech. Great discoveries are of little benefit if no one else can learn about them.

About 400 colleges and universities offer a bachelor's degree in geology. Students studying for this major devote about one-fourth of their time to geology courses such as physical, structural, and historical geology, mineralogy, petrology, and paleontology. About one-third of their course work is in the basic sciences such as chemistry, physics, and biology; mathematics, including statistics, calculus, differential equations, and computer science; and engineering. The remainder of their study time is engaged in English and composition courses, history and economics, foreign language, and other academic subjects.

More than 160 universities award advanced degrees in geology. Graduate students take advanced courses in geology and specialize in one branch of the science. Students seeking the doctorate do a research dissertation project under the guidance of expert faculty members.

In many of the industrial and government jobs in geology, a person with a bachelor's or master's degree will be specially trained on the job in the unique skills necessary for that occupation. Often, part-time studies leading to a graduate degree are paid for by the employer to enhance the knowledge and usefulness of the scientist.

Geologists usually begin their careers in field exploration or as research assistants in laboratories. With experience, they can be promoted to project leader, program manager, or other management and research positions.

Students planning careers in exploration geology and in some of the other fields where vigorous mountaineering, hiking, or other scouting-type skills are needed should like the outdoors and must have physical stamina.

What Are My Chances of Getting a Job as a Geologist?

Employment opportunities in geology, as in the other sciences and all professions, vary with the general economic climate of the country and with the nation's needs. The long-range picture looks very good. Dwindling energy, mineral, and water resources, increasing environmental concerns, a better use of land, and a need for better waste disposal systems present new challenges to our society. The geologist will serve a special and important function in reaching an energy-independent, ecologically balanced future in the twenty-first century.

The employment of geologists is expected to grow faster than the average for all occupations through the mid-1980's. Over 2,300 new jobs for geologists are expected each year.

The demand for qualified women geologists is very high, and there is no reason why women should not find a geological career extremely rewarding. There are also very few minority groups represented in the occupation. Therefore, many employers are actively recruiting females and minority earth scientists.

If you are interested in geology but would prefer not being a scientist, there are jobs for technical writers and librarians with specialized training in geology. In addition, careers in law or business frequently can be strengthened by a background in geology.

The increased prices for petroleum and the necessity to locate new sources of other minerals as older sources become exhausted will require many new geologists. Additional geologists also will be needed to develop new resources, such as geothermal energy. This, in turn, should require that colleges and universities, which are not hiring many new geology faculty at this time, begin recruiting new instructional staff. The interest in energy resources may also spark school boards into creating new curricula in the earth sciences, which will need trained faculty.

How Much Do Geologists Earn?

Geologists have relatively high salaries. In 1978 average starting salaries for geologists with bachelor's degrees were over $16,500. Graduates with master's degrees started over $20,000. A geologist with a doctorate could expect a starting salary over $25,000.

Salaries for geologists with experience are, of course, much higher. The average salary for geologists employed in the Federal government was over $27,000 a year in 1978. The salary for many geologists working for oil companies may be ten or fifteen thousand dollars a year higher than that figure.

In addition to the financial rewards, the work of a geologist is often very rewarding and enjoyable. A geologist derives great pleasure and inner satisfaction from the many hours spent in solving the puzzles of the earth's composition, structure, and history.

The conditions of work for a geologist vary. Exploration geologists often work overseas, meaning separation from their families for periods of time. This work, however, is exciting, as well as providing an opportunity to visit exotic lands. Geologists in the U.S., too, often have to travel to remote sites by helicopter and jeep and cover large areas on foot. Geologists in mining sometimes work underground. Others work in comfortable, well-lighted, well-ventilated offices and laboratories.

Where Can I Obtain Training in Geology?

Some of the colleges and universities that offer a major in geology are:

> University of Alabama, University, Alabama 35486
> Allegheny College, Meadville, Pennsylvania 16335
> University of Arkansas, Fayetteville, Arkansas 72701
> Boston College, Chestnut Hill, Massachusetts 02167
> Brown University, Providence, Rhode Island 02912
> University of Colorado, Boulder, Colorado 80302
> Dartmouth College, Hanover, New Hampshire 03755
> University of Dayton, Dayton, Ohio 45469
> Dickinson College, Carlisle, Pennsylvania 17013
> Hofstra University, Hempstead, New York 11550

Indiana State University, Terre Haute, Indiana 47809
University of Iowa, Iowa City, Iowa 52242
University of Kentucky, Lexington, Kentucky 40506
Long Island University, Brooklyn, N.Y. 11201
Marshall University, Huntington, West Virginia 25705
University of Miami, Coral Gables, Florida 33124
Michigan State University, East Lansing, Michigan 48824
University of Montana, Missoula, Montana 59801
University of Nevada, Las Vegas, Nevada 89109
New Mexico Institute of Mining and Technology. Socorro, New Mexico 87801
University of North Dakota, Grand Forks, North Dakota 58201
Ohio State University, Columbus, Ohio 43212
Ohio University, Athens, Ohio 45701
Pennsylvania State University, University Park, Pennsylvania 16802
University of Rochester, Rochester, New York 14627
Smith College, Northampton, Massachusetts 01060
St. Louis University, St. Louis, Missouri 63103
Stanford University, Stanford, California 94305
Temple University, Philadelphia, Pennsylvania 19122
Texas A & M University, College Station, Texas 77843
University of Toledo, Toledo, Ohio 43614
Tulane University, New Orleans, Louisiana 70118
Utah State University, Logan, Utah 84322
Virginia Polytechnical Institute, Blacksburg, Virginia 24061
West Virginia University, Morgantown, West Virginia 26506
Western State College, Gunnison, Colorado 81230
College of William and Mary, Williamsburg, Virginia 23185
Williams College, Williamstown, Massachusetts 01267

Where Can I Get More Information About Geology?

For additional information write to:

The American Geological Institute
5205 Leesburg Pike
Falls Church, VA 22041

For information about Federal government jobs in geology, write to:

U.S. Civil Service Commission
1900 E Street, N.W.
Washington, DC 20415

For detailed information about the field, read:
Your Future in Geology by Joseph L. Weitz. Richards Rosen Press, Inc.

GEOPHYSICS

Geophysics is the application of physics, chemistry, and mathematics to the problems and processes of the earth. Geophysicists study the causes and outcomes of natural upheavals such as earthquakes and volcanoes. They investigate the magnetic and gravitational forces of the earth. They measure the size and shape of the earth's surface, and they try to locate areas where rich mineral and fuel deposits can be found. The upper atmosphere, the ionosphere, the sun, and the solar system are areas of interest to the geophysicist.

Geophysics is usually divided into three general areas: solid earth geophysics, fluid earth geophysics, and upper atmosphere geophysics. Geophysicists usually specialize in one of these three fields.

Solid earth geophysicists search for oil and mineral deposits, map the earth's surface, and study earthquakes. They are concerned with the geologic and planetary aspects of the earth.

Fluid earth geophysicists study the distribution, circulation, and physical properties of underground and surface waters, including glaciers, snow, and permafrost (the perennially frozen subsoil of the Arctic tundra). The fluid earth geophysicists are concerned with how rainfall permeates the soil and its effect on water supply, irrigation, flooding, and soil erosion.

Upper atmosphere geophysicists study the earth's magnetic and electric fields. They compare their findings with those from other planets to learn about the history and composition of the solar system. Their research enables meteorologists to make better predictions concerning the weather.

Some questions geophysicists are trying to answer are:

How do conditions in the upper atmosphere affect radio and television transmission?
Why is the pull of gravity greater at the poles than at the equator?
What is the inside of the earth like?
Can earthquakes be predicted?
What was the earth like a billion years ago?
How can fresh water be preserved?
Why is the Martian landscape much like that of the moon, but with evidence of ancient water flow?
What are the forces that permit mountains to rise and continents to drift apart?

Geophysics is one of the earth sciences. It uses basic scientific principles to study the earth's crust, atmosphere, and water flow. Most of its efforts today are directed toward finding new oil-producing areas. The study of geophysical problems requires a good foundation in chemistry, physics, and mathematics.

What Do Geophysicists Do?

Geophysicists study the earth with highly complex instruments such as the magnetometer, which measures variations in the earth's magnetic field; the gravimeter, which measures minute changes in the earth's gravitational attraction; seismographs, which measure the sound waves produced by earthquakes and other disturbances beneath the earth's surface; and satellites, which conduct tests in outer space. The computer, as in all the other sciences today, is a basic tool required for collecting and analyzing data.

The American Geophysical Union, an organization of geophysicists and other scientists who study the earth, is divided into several sections each covering an important area of research. A brief description of these areas follows:

Geodesy is the study of the size, shape, and gravitational field of the earth. The principal task of *geodesists* is the precise measurement of the earth's surface. They use high-flying aircraft and satellites to determine the positions, elevations, and distances between points on the earth.

Geodesists establish observation points all over the earth's surface. This network of points is used for extremely accurate mapping of the elevation of the land above sea level, as well as for the exact location of the point in respect to its latitude and longitude. Geodetic survey maps, which are usually produced by Federal and local government geodesists, are used by farmers, land developers, mining companies, and homeowners to better understand the physical characteristics of the land they own or intend to use.

Gravitational studies of various regions of the earth by geodesists give us insight into the variations in the earth's crust. These measurements can aid in oil exploration and in surveying for such natural resources as iron ore, natural gas, and salt.

Seismology is the study of earthquakes, both natural and man-made. Most of what we know about the interior of the earth has been learned by *seismologists* studying the behavior of shock waves from large earthquakes and from dynamite explosions set off underground. By studying the shocks from small explosions in the ocean, they have learned about the ocean depths and the structures of the layers below the seafloor.

Seismological studies are used to explore for oil and minerals. Sound waves travel faster through hard rock than through soft coal, and they travel very slowly through liquid pools of oil and gaseous buildups of methane. Therefore, by carefully detonating small explosions in deep wells, these scientists can investigate subsurface land formations quickly and inexpensively.

About 5,000 earthquakes a year occur around the globe. Most are too minor to be felt by any but the most sensitive machines. Seismologists study these quakes to discover ways that might be used to predict when major quakes may happen.

Seismological studies are gaining important recognition through the efforts of groups who point out the hazards involved in locating certain nuclear power plants near faults below the surface. Seismologists also are able to detect underground atomic bomb explosions occurring in foreign countries.

Geomagnetism or the magnetic field of the earth has been studied for hundreds of years. Christopher Columbus never would have attempted his voyage if it hadn't been for the then recently discovered magnetic compass. However, even today we have only crude explanations for this phenomenon.

The earth's magnetic field originates deep within its core of iron and nickel compressed under millions of tons of pressure, and it extends far into space. It interacts both with magnetic minerals of various rocks and with the magnetic fields of the sun, the moon, and other intergalactic bodies to create the magnetosphere far out in space.

The measurement and study of these interactions require the efforts of many earth scientists. Specialists in this field are called *geomagnetic physicists.*

The magnetic properties of some kinds of rocks tell scientists how the earth's magnetic field has changed over the last three billion years. These scientists, called *paleomagnetic* ("paleo-" means old) *geophysicists,* have discovered that a rock's magnetic field was lined up with the earth's magnetic field when the rock solidified from lava or magma. By studying this "fossil" magnetism, we can learn about shifts in the ocean floor, continental drift, and how the north and south pole have wandered since the planet's creation. Their discoveries are a part of the new field called *plate tectonics.*

The magnetic field of the earth controls the motion of the earth's ionosphere. This region of electrons and ions is formed by solar X-rays and ultraviolet rays colliding with the rarefied gases in the upper atmosphere. Disruptions in the ionosphere affect communication system transmissions and weather and result in the spectacular light emissions called the aurora borealis.

Accurate measurements of the earth's magnetic field continue at a network of geomagnetic stations around the globe. These were first established in 1882. Their results are continuously fed into computers, which plot the earth's ever-changing characteristics.

Vulcanology is the study of volcanoes. It also involves the study of all the forces and processes of the molten, flowing rock that lies only a few miles beneath the surface of any spot on earth. This thermal structure of the earth deposits the ores and forms the rocks that are used by industry. *Volcanologists* investigate the causes of volcanoes and try to predict when major eruptions may take place. Volcanologists are also trying to find ways of tapping the tremendous subterranean heat for use as an energy resource.

Petrology is the study of the classification and composition of rocks. Some rocks are over three billion years old. How did they form? How do we know how old a rock is? How was the rock made? How are different kinds of rocks distributed over the earth? These are questions the *petrologists* are trying to solve. The solution to these problems will provide a geochronology, a time scale of geological events, which will help us understand the physical and chemical evolution of the earth.

Geochemists study the chemical composition of the various components of the earth. They are trying to discover the conditions that caused one kind of metal, such as tin, to be deposited in one place while another, such as iron, is found somewhere else. Geochemical studies help mineral and fuel companies to determine the deposits in various areas that might be profitable for development.

Hydrologists study the occurrence, behavior, and distribution of water in all its forms on and in the earth. The water cycle, evaporation-precipitation-condensation, is the means by which vegetation and animals, including us, are provided with fresh water, which is becoming increasingly difficult to obtain.

Hydrologists study the watersheds, or freshwater runoff areas, for rivers and streams. If a forest is destroyed by natural or man-made forces, its ability to hold and distribute fresh water may be lost. This erosion can seriously affect the down-river communities that rely on a constant supply. Most fresh water is not flowing above ground, but is found in underground streams, rivers, and rivulets as well as in the soil. This resource must be carefully preserved, and much research is needed to locate and maintain this storage area.

The deltas of Mississippi and of Egypt are formed by soil deposited by mighty rivers. This enriched land is used by farmers to provide abundant harvests. Small changes in the flow of the river could bring devastation in the form of drought or flood, which could seriously disrupt the life of the region. More than ten billion dollars a year is spent on hydrologic projects to bring water to cities and crops and to preserve and purify this necessary resource.

Hydrologists also investigate glaciers, ice, snow, and permafrost. They carry out their studies around the globe. Their work is important to agriculture, forestry, biology, and all the other earth sciences.

Technophysics is one of the newest branches of geophysics. It involves a study of how the earth's crust has moved and changed since it solidified from cosmic material about five billion years ago. The seafloor is spreading, causing down-warping trenches that are the deepest recesses in the earth. A generally accepted theory that a huge single continent split up millions of years ago, creating today's seven continents, is being studied by *technophysicists*. They are investigating fossil and rock formations that are similar in both western Africa and eastern Brazil, which are shaped like two jigsaw puzzle pieces that can easily be fitted together.

Technophysicists are trying to discover the forces that produce these changes and their effects on vulcanology and seismology. The San Andreas fault in California may be caused by these continental shifts, and an understanding of the principles involved can provide methods for easing the pressures slowly, so that a major earthquake may be avoided.

Exploration geophysicists are the scientists who find the geological conditions that might indicate valuable oil, natural gas, or mineral deposits below the surface. They do not drill the wells, nor dig into the earth; instead they carefully study and survey an area with gravimeters, magnetometers, portable seismographs, and other delicate equipment and predict whether the area is worth further investigation.

Nearly one billion dollars a year is spent on geophysical exploration for new oil reserves. In addition, the exploration geophysicists search for radioactive ores for atomic energy, as well as new deposits of iron ore, copper, tin, zinc, and other metals.

Planetology is the most recent occupation in geophysics. It is the physical and chemical study of the moon, the other planets, and other massive bodies in the solar system. *Planetologists* compare their data with information about the earth so that scientists can learn more about the origin, history, and structure of our planet. Planetologists use radiation data, spectroscopy, gathered by earthbound instruments and information recorded by satellites which "fly past" the planets and their moons. Space vehicles have actually landed on the moon, Mars, and Venus. Scoops of soil have been analyzed, and moon rocks have been brought back to earth. Someday we may be mining the planets and asteroids in our solar system. Scientists may inhabit them to learn more about the universe and to find ways to make life on earth more satisfying and productive.

Where Are Geophysicists Employed?

About 12,000 people worked as geophysicists in 1976. Most worked in private industry, chiefly for petroleum and natural gas companies. Others are in mining companies, exploration and consulting firms, and research institutes. A few are independent consultants, and some do geophysical prospecting on a fee or contract basis.

Geophysicists are employed in many Southwestern and Western states and in those on the Gulf Coast, where large oil and natural gas fields are located.

Many geophysicists work in offices in large metropolitan regions, where they use computers to help them analyze the data sent from all regions of the globe and from outer space. Some geophysicists work in laboratories, where they analyze samples to learn their composition.

Some laboratories try to recreate the conditions that cause geologic changes so that the scientists can find ways to predict where oil fields might be, how earthquakes damage buildings, how water is stored in various kinds of soils, and so on. Computer simulation is a new and powerful technique for carrying out "experiments" with the earth that could never actually be performed.

Most geophysicists, at some point in their career or training, carry out field work, which may be in any portion of the world, on land, at sea, in the air, or, for some, in outer space. Often the choice of the area rests with the scientist. Many request foreign work where they can explore deserts, jungles, and mountains as well as visit exotic cities.

Almost 25 percent of all geophysicists work for the Federal government. Many are assigned to jobs in and around Washington, D.C., and in Denver, Colorado, where the National Oceanic and Atmospheric Administration has a large headquarters. The U.S. Geological Survey has offices around the U.S., and geophysicists work for the Defense Department at bases around the globe. Other geophysicists work for colleges and universities, state governments, and nonprofit research institutions.

Geophysicists usually begin their careers as trainees after graduating from college. Trainees learn to handle the sophisticated electronic equipment used by geophysicists. They learn to record data, feed it into the computers, and interpret the results. Trainees work in the field and become familiar with all phases of the operation. This on-the-job training enhances the skills the scientist learned at college and teaches him or her the special requirements of the firm that is paying for the job.

How Can I Become a Geophysicist?

A bachelor's degree with a major in geophysics or a geophysical specialty is the usual requirement for beginning jobs in the field. About 50 colleges and universities award the bachelor's degree in geophysics. Other colleges, although not specifically offering geophysics degrees, give bachelor's degrees in such fields as geophysical engineering, petroleum geology, and geodesy. Many colleges offer programs in earth science or geology that may prepare a student for a career in geophysics.

Some beginning jobs in geophysics are available for people with bachelor's degrees in related disciplines such as chemistry, physics, engineering, or mathematics, who also have taken coursework, or minored, in geophysics.

Research and supervisory jobs in geophysics usually require graduate training. A master's degree or a doctorate is often a prerequisite for any high-level job. About 60 universities grant graduate degrees in geophysics. Often a person who studies geophysics in graduate school may have an undergraduate degree in another branch of the sciences or in mathematics.

If you want to become a geophysicist, you should take a strong college-preparatory program in high school. You will need biology, chemistry, and physics. If your school offers earth science, astronomy, or oceanography, you should take these courses, too, but only in addition to the biology, chemistry, and physics. You will need a lot of mathematics in geophysics. Take intermediate algebra, trigonometry, and geometry. If you can take a course in calculus, that will help. Certainly, take a course in computer science, if available.

English and social studies courses will prepare you with the communications skills and historical background you will need to be an effective scientist. Geophysicists often travel and work in countries around the world; therefore, a knowledge of one or more modern foreign languages is very helpful.

In college the geophysics major usually takes calculus, physics, chemistry and introductory geophysics courses during his first two years, along with coursework in English composition, foreign languages, psychology, economics, and so on. In his or her junior and senior year, the coursework will be specialized and may include geochemistry, geophysical methods, electromagnetism, engineering, and so on.

In graduate school the geophysics major will take courses in his or her particular field of interest such as seismology, vulcanology, hydrology, geodesy. For a Ph.D., the student must do an original research project in geophysics, and prepare a dissertation. This work is sponsored by a committee of professors who are experts in their field.

Many geophysicists enter the field with a bachelor's degree and attend graduate school part time. Often this training is paid for by the company for which the scientist works.

What Are My Chances of Getting a Job as a Geophysicist?

The employment outlook for graduates in the field of geophysics is excellent. The energy crisis has created a need in this very specialized field. The Federal government in the mid-1970's predicted that there would be about 800 openings a year for geophysicists. However, the need has significantly increased.

It is very important to realize that few qualified people enter the field each year. Fewer than 200 graduates a year are trained in geophysics. It is an occupation requiring a very special set of interests and skills, and many people are neither qualified nor adept at developing these abilities.

Employment in geophysics will grow much faster than the average for all occupations in the 1980's. As known deposits of petroleum and other minerals are depleted, petroleum and mining companies will need increasing numbers of geophysicists who can use sophisticated electronic techniques to find less accessible fuel and mineral deposits.

In addition, geophysicists with advanced training will be needed to do research on radioactivity, cosmic and solar radiation, geothermal (heat from inside the earth) and tidal power, and so on to find new resources of energy for generating electricity.

The Federal government is preparing to spend billions of dollars to aid research in geophysics, and many new jobs should be opening in this important field.

How Much Do Geophysicists Earn?

Men and women in geophysics are well paid. Starting salaries are equal to those offered any engineer or science graduate. The industry provides a good future and will continue to offer salaries that will keep pace with the increased cost of living.

In general, the higher the degree the person has received, the larger his starting income. Most geophysical and oil companies offer fringe benefits in addition to good salaries; they often include life and health insurance, retirement programs, and profit sharing plans. It is not unusual for a geophysicist to become part owner of the company for which he works, or to receive a substantial bonus for helping to find a rich field.

In the Federal government in 1978, geophysicists having a bachelor's degree could begin at about $11,000. Geophysicists with a master's degree could start at around $15,000, and those with a doctorate could start at around $24,000. In 1978 the average salary for geophysicists employed by the Federal government was $28,632.

In private industry in 1978 graduates with bachelor's degrees started at an average of about $16,500 a year, and those with master's degrees started at around $18,000. Salaries in private industry may climb faster than those in government as the need for geophysicists increases and the profits of the oil companies rise.

Many geophysicists work outdoors and must be willing to travel for extended periods of time. Some work at research stations in remote areas or aboard ships and aircraft equipped with sophisticated geophysical equipment. When not in the field, geophysicists work in modern, well-equipped, well-lighted laboratories and offices.

Where Can I Obtain Training in Geophysics?

Some of the colleges and universities that offer a major in geophysics are:

University of Alabama, University, Alabama 35486
Baylor University, Waco, Texas 76703

Bowling Green State University, Bowling Green, Ohio 43403
University of Chicago, Chicago, Illinois 60637
Colgate University, Hamilton, New York 13346
Colorado School of Mines, Golden, Colorado 80401
De Pauw University, Greencastle, Indiana 46135
Duquesne University, Pittsburgh, Pennsylvania 15219
Harvard University, Cambridge, Massachusetts 02138
University of Houston, Houston, Texas 77004
Johns Hopkins University, Baltimore, Maryland 21218
Louisiana Technical University, Ruston, Louisiana 71270
Michigan State University, East Lansing, Michigan 48824
Michigan Tech University, Houghton, Michigan 49931
Northwestern University, Evanston, Illinois 60201
Pennsylvania State University, University Park, Pennsylvania 16802
Purdue University, Fort Wayne, Indiana 46805
Rice University, Houston, Texas 77001
St. Lawrence University, Canton, New York 13617
Stanford University, Stanford, California 94305
State University of New York, Stony Brook, New York 11790
Stevens Institute of Technology, Hoboken, New Jersey 07030
Texas A & M University, College Station, Texas 77843
Tulane University, New Orleans, Louisiana 70118
University of Tulsa, Tulsa, Oklahoma 74104
Virginia Polytechnical Institute, Blacksburg, Virginia 24061
Wesleyan University, Middletown, Connecticut 06457
Wittenberg University, Springfield, Ohio 45501

Where Can I Get More Information About Geophysics?

For further information on careers in geophysics write to:

Society of Exploration Geophysicists
P.O. Box 3098
Tulsa, OK 74101

American Geophysical Union
1909 K Street, N.W.
Washington, DC 20006

For information about jobs in the Federal government, write to:

U.S. Civil Service Commission
1900 E Street, N.W.
Washington, DC 20250

For detailed information about the field read:

Your Future in Geology by Joseph L. Weitz. Richards Rosen Press.

METEOROLOGY

Meteorology is the study of the atmosphere and the weather. Meteorologists observe weather conditions around the globe, try to understand what caused their development, and try to predict what the weather is going to do next. Meteorology involves the use of chemistry, physics, mathematics, geology, oceanography, and other sciences. Meteorologists try to answer such questions as:

Is it possible to moderate the force of a hurricane or to alter its course?

Can clouds be controlled to bring rain to barren places?

How far in advance can local weather forecasts be accurately made?

How can we control air pollution?

What are the effects of cities and large factories on the weather?

How can buildings be made safe from severe weather?

How can space exploration help weather prediction on the earth?

As you probably know, the suffix "ology" means "study of." The prefix "meteor" means heavenly or celestial. Historically, meteorology was a study of the sky, and we know today that our weather is directly influenced by the major object in the sky, our sun. The sun supplies the energy for the water cycle, which continuously produces evaporation of water from the oceans, rain over the land, and the watershedding of streams and rivers across the land. The sun and the moon produce the gravitational pulls that attract the oceans' tides. The heating of the atmosphere produces the high- and low-pressure areas that cause the wind patterns, which in turn blow the clouds over the earth and the waves upon the seas.

The study of weather, as you can see, is very complex. A great deal of physics is involved in explaining and interpreting the causes and movements of weather fronts. Chemistry is needed for interpreting the crystallizing forces within a cloud, or the effects of pollutants on the atmosphere. And, of course, mathematics and computer science are of utmost value to the meteorologist.

What Do Meteorologists Do?

Meteorologists perform different tasks on different jobs. The biggest employer of meteorologists is the National Weather Service, which is part of the National Oceanic and Atmospheric Administration (NOAA) of the U.S. Department of Commerce. Meteorologists at the Weather Service constantly observe the weather and continuously record the temperature, humidity, barometric pressure, wind velocity, pollutants, spores (for hay fever sufferers), and other variables in the air. These meteorologists may work in office buildings in major cities; in laboratories on remote islands, deserts, or mountain ranges; on ships cruising the oceans; at airports; or in aircraft flying throughout the troposphere and the lower stratosphere. The conditions of the upper stratosphere are studied by scientists with weather balloons and rockets.

Satellites, such as the TIROS and NIMBUS, send global weather data to U.S. tracking stations positioned around the world. On the six o'clock news we can see satellite weather photographs of huge storm fronts moving across the continental United States.

The data collected from these weather observers are sent to weather analysts and forecasters at centrally located bureaus. These highly skilled specialists chart the isolated data on weather maps and feed the information into high-speed computers. It is their job to predict what the weather will be like for your home town, for farmers, for pilots, for sea captains, for sporting events, and so on.

Weather forecasters and observers are on the job around the clock, every day of the year. They must have a careful and inquiring mind and the desire to do the best possible job. They must be especially reliable. Their reports often go unchecked, and the information may be responsible for the lives of many people. For example, careless weather observations have led to airplane accidents.

Meteorologists who specialize in forecasting the weather are known professionally as *synoptic meteorologists.* They are the largest group of specialists.

Some meteorologists are engaged in basic and applied research. *Physical meteorologists* study the chemical and electrical properties of the atmosphere. They do research on the effect of the atmosphere on transmission of light, sound, and radio waves. They investigate the factors that form clouds, hurricanes, and rain. They are concerned with the effect of pollutants, such as fluorochlorocarbons from aerosol sprays, on the upper atmosphere. This pollutant causes the ozone, which absorbs dangerous ultraviolet radiation from the sun, to break down into regular oxygen, which cannot protect us from this radiation. They are also concerned with factory and car emissions that combine with rain to form acids, which fall on our crops, wildlife, and cities. "Acid rains" and gaseous pollutants have enveloped the earth and have been found in the most remote regions of the arctic wastelands.

Climatologists are meteorologists who study climatic trends and analyze historical records on wind, rainfall, sunshine, and temperature to determine the general patterns of weather that have occurred over an area for an extended period of time. Climate is the average weather condition over several years (or even several centuries). Before city planners, major builders, or agricultural conglomerates begin a costly project, they want to know how much rain an area normally gets, how the temperature varies, whether the area is subject to tornadoes or floods, and so on. Climatologists are trying to discover the prehistoric conditions that led to a tropical forest over what is now New Jersey,

A technical staffer measures the rates at which chemical reactions occur in contaminated atmospheres, as well as the concentrations of specific contaminants.

and to the ice ages that covered Europe and most of North America with continental glaciers. They are investigating whether the earth is getting warmer on an annual basis, or colder. And they are concerned with the effects on the earth's climate of smoke and carbon dioxide from hydrocarbon exhausts.

Other meteorologists apply their training to specific problems. Some work in aerospace engineering, where they aid in the design of aircraft and spacecraft. Some specialize in agriculture, where they help farmers adapt their crops and methods to changing weather patterns. Droughts and storms have ruined millions of acres of farmland over the last few decades, and *agricultural meteorologists* are trying to understand these conditions and find ways to prevent or, at least, cope with them.

Biometeorologists study the effects of the atmosphere on living things. They are interested in how weather changes cause physiological and psychological changes in man and other species. Some biometeorologists have theories that connect air pressure abnormalities with general feelings of anxiety and uneasiness among a population. In other words, they think that on days when "everybody" seems irritable, there might be a weather or pollution factor influencing a city. Others have found that certain animal species react differently days before a hurricane approaches, although the general weather conditions appear unaffected.

Civil engineers work with specially trained meteorologists in designing buildings, piers, beachfronts, dams, and so on that can withstand prevalent weather conditions. Electrical engineers and communications specialists also work with meteorologists who are familiar with how the atmosphere affects radio waves, radar, and television signals.

Paleoclimatology is the study of early climates. Geologists working with these scientists may be able to find oil and natural gas fields, since these fuels were formed from tropical forests that were heaved underground millions of years ago.

Meteorologists also work for broadcasting stations and news media. Their weather reports are seen by millions, who plan their picnics, parades, trips, and clothing on the forecasts. Sometimes actors or models merely present the reports from the National Weather Service. But more often the personalities are highly trained meteorologists who try to interpret the weather conditions for the public, and stress the ever-changing factors that can cause a prediction for a sunny day to end up as a six-hour thunderstorm.

About one-third of all civilian meteorologists work primarily in weather forecasting and measurement, and another one-third work in research and development. About one-fifth of all civilians in this occupation work as administrators and in management positions.

Some meteorologists teach and do research in colleges and universities. Some teach earth science in secondary school systems. In institutions without separate meteorology or earth science departments, they may teach geography, mathematics, physics, chemistry, or geology as well as meteorology.

Where Are Meteorologists Employed?

In 1976 there were only 5,500 meteorologists employed in the U.S. In addition to these civilian meteorologists, thousands of members of the Army, Navy, Air Force, and Coast Guard did forecasting and other meteorological work.

The largest employer of civilian meteorologists was the National Oceanic and Atmospheric Administration. Over 2,100 scientists worked at stations in all parts of the U.S. and in a small number of foreign countries in 1978. The Department of Defense employed over 200 meteorologists.

Other meteorologists who worked for the Federal government worked at the Department of Energy, the National Aeronautics and Space Administration, the Federal Aviation Administration, the Department of Agriculture, and the Department of Health and Human Services.

Almost 2,000 meteorologists worked for private enterprise. Commercial airlines employed several hundred to forecast weather along flight routes and to brief pilots on weather conditions. Others worked for the aerospace industry aiding in the design of aircraft and space vehicles that would fly through the atmosphere and its weather. They worked for communications and broadcasting companies, helping them send better signals and reporting the weather. Transportation companies and energy corporations need meteorologists to help with the routing of shipments and energy resources. Merchants and the food industry rely on their own meteorologists to supply accurate, pertinent information for protecting the shipment of perishable goods and for planting and harvesting produce. Also, some meteorologists work as private consultants and for private research organizations.

BELL LABS

High-frequency signals beamed to this antenna from Comstar satellites are enabling Bell Labs to study signal attenuation caused by atmospheric conditions. Such research may prove useful for design of future satellite transmissions systems.

Beginning meteorologists often start in jobs involving routine data collection, computation, or analysis. Experienced meteorologists may advance to supervisory or administrative jobs. A few well-qualified meteorologists with a background in science, engineering, and business administration may establish their own weather consulting services.

How Can I Become a Meteorologist?

A bachelor's degree with a major in meteorology is the usual minimum requirement for beginning jobs in weather forecasting. However, a bachelor's degree in a related science or engineering, along with some courses in meteorology, is acceptable for some jobs. For example, the Federal government's minimum requirement for beginning jobs is a bachelor's degree with at least 20 semester hours of study in meteorology and courses in physics and mathematics, including calculus. However, employers prefer to hire those with an advanced degree, and an advanced degree is increasingly necessary for advancement.

When you are in high school, you should take a well-balanced college preparatory program. Mathematics is the principal tool of the meteorologist. You should study as much of it as possible. Intermediate algebra is essential. To succeed in meteorology, you should find mathematics relatively interesting and not too hard. Geometry and trigonometry courses will help you prepare for your career. Computer training, if available, will be very helpful.

Since meteorology involves international cooperation, knowledge of French, German, Russian, or Chinese will help you considerably. A candidate with ability in one of these languages will have a much better chance of obtaining a job.

English is, of course, absolutely necessary. You must be able to communicate accurately and easily in both writing and speaking. You should be able to describe events logically, clearly, and completely.

The prediction of weather involves a thorough knowledge of the chemistry and physics of the atmosphere and its interaction with land and sea. In high school you should study both chemistry and physics. If earth science is offered, use it as an additional elective, but do not substitute it for either chemistry or physics. Biology is necessary for understanding the ecological and natural influences of weather.

In college you have to decide if you want to major in meteorology or major in another science field with meteorology as your minor. In 1978 there were more than 50 universities and colleges in the U.S. and Canada offering the bachelor's degree in meteorology. The principal advantage in majoring in meteorology as an undergraduate is that you may go to work as a meteorologist directly upon graduation. You will be able to begin a career, but you will probably lack enough training in physics, chemistry, and advanced mathematics to engage in any research.

To prepare for a research specialization, you may continue your education at the graduate level, or you may study advanced physics or mathematics in college while taking meteorological course work. A number of interesting and valuable interdisciplinary careers become accessible if you combine a degree in meteorology with a degree in another major subject. Joint degrees with meteorology have been awarded in aerospace engineering, agriculture, astronomy, biology, civil and environmental engineering, electrical engineering, geology, journalism, communications, mathematics, and oceanography. People with these backgrounds can expect interesting jobs and have allowed themselves the opportunity to change occupations or select new careers as they move up the career ladder or as opportunities afford themselves.

Meteorology training has been effectively combined with law, medicine, speech, and business administration. Physics and chemistry have proved to be the most fruitful of all the interdisciplinary areas. Scientists with extensive training in these fields have contributed to major advances in our understanding of the atmosphere. The meteorological satellites and the man-in-space program are outstanding examples of career activities involving various aspects of science and engineering.

Some respected research meteorologists and teachers think that it may be best not to major in meteorology until graduate school. They feel that rigorous training in the traditional sciences and mathematics is the best preparation for today's jobs in weather forecasting.

Advanced work requires a master's degree or doctorate. More than 55 colleges in the United States and Canada offer graduate work through the doctorate in meteorology and closely allied fields. Doctoral work requires difficult, advanced training and an original research project that will culminate in a dissertation on your contribution to the understanding of the atmosphere. Many meteorologists study for their graduate degrees under work-study or part-time arrangements with their employers.

An excellent way to receive training in meteorology is through the armed services. The U.S. Army, Air Force, and Navy have extensive meteorological facilities staffed by persons whom they have trained. These services offer special programs often in affiliation with degree-granting universities, where you can obtain meteorological skills and a degree while serving your tour of duty.

What Are My Chances of Getting a Job as a Meteorologist?

There should be about 200 openings a year for meteorologists. Although the number of new jobs created by growth in the occupation and the openings due to replacement needs is relatively small, the number of persons obtaining degrees in meteorology also is small. If trends in the number of degrees granted continue, the number of people seeking entry to the field will about equal the requirements.

Employment in the field is expected to increase about 15 to 25 percent over the next ten years. Jobs in industry and in weather consulting firms are expected to grow as these concerns discover how people trained in meteorology can help them meet clean air standards and increase production.

The aviation industry and the aerospace projects may need additional meteorologists as their importance grows in the 1980's. There should also be some openings in radio and television as local stations are finding that trained meteorologists present better weather reporting than actors who must rely on weather service reports that may be several hours behind a developing weather situation.

Colleges and universities will offer some job opportunities, but only for those meteorologists with advanced degrees. Secondary schools, too, should have some new jobs as earth science and environmental science become more popular. Jobs in the secondary schools will require some specialized training in teaching. Also, as in the community college, and perhaps in the university, meteorological faculty may well be expected to teach courses in physics, mathematics, and other allied fields.

The employment of civilian meteorologists in the Federal government is not expected to grow significantly in the next decade, although there will be openings created by replacement needs.

How Much Do Meteorologists Earn?

Meteorologists have relatively high earnings. The starting salary for those in the Federal government with a bachelor's degree in 1978 was about $11,000; for those with a master's degree, around $15,000; and for those with a doctorate, around $24,000. The average salary for a meteorologist in the government was $28,565 in 1978.

The average salary for all meteorologists (most meteorologists have more than 10 years' experience and have graduate training) was estimated to be $27,000 in 1978. Meteorologists with a B.S. degree earned $23,000 on the average; those with an M.S. degree, $29,000; and with a Ph.D., $33,000.

Jobs for meteorologists in weather stations, which are operated around the clock every day of the year, often involve night work and rotating shifts. Most stations are at airports or in or near cities; some are in isolated and remote areas. Some meteorologists work alone, but most work as part of a team.

Where Can I Obtain Training in Meteorology?

Some of the colleges and universities that offer a major in meteorology are:

Colorado State University, Fort Collins, Colorado 80523
Columbia University, New York, New York 10027
Drexel University, Philadelphia, Pennsylvania 19104
Florida State University, Tallahassee, Florida 32306
Georgia Institute of Technology, Atlanta, Georgia 30332
Harvard University, Cambridge, Massachusetts 02138
Johns Hopkins University, Baltimore, Maryland 21218
Massachusetts Institute of Technology, Cambridge, Massachusetts 02139
McGill University, Quebec, Canada H3C 3G1
Montana State University, Bozeman, Montana 59717

New Mexico Institute of Mining and Technology, Socorro, New Mexico 87801
Ohio State University, Columbus, Ohio 43210
Oregon State University, Corvallis, Oregon 97331
Pennsylvania State University–University Park Campus, University Park, Pennsylvania 16802
Princeton University, Princeton, New Jersey 08544
Purdue University, West Lafayette, Indiana 47907
Rice University, Houston, Texas 77001
Rutgers University, New Brunswick, New Jersey 08903
Saint Louis University, St. Louis, Missouri 63108
San Jose State University, San Jose, California 95912
South Dakota School of Mines and Technology, Rapid City, South Dakota, 57701
Stanford University, Stanford, California 94305
State University of New York at Albany, Albany, New York 12222
State University of New York at Stony Brook, Stony Brook, New York 11794
Texas A&M University, College Station, Texas 77843
Trenton State College, Trenton, New Jersey 08625
University of Alaska, Fairbanks, Alaska 99701
University of Alberta, Edmonton, Alberta, Canada T6G 2G1
University of Arizona, Tucson, Arizona 85721
University of California, Berkeley, Berkeley, California 94720
University of California, Los Angeles, Los Angeles, California 90024
University of California, San Diego, San Diego, California 92093
University of Chicago, Chicago, Illinois 60637
University of Colorado, Boulder, Colorado 80309
University of Florida, Gainesville, Florida 32611
University of Hawaii at Manoa, Honolulu, Hawaii 96822
University of Maryland at College Park, College Park, Maryland 20742
University of Miami, Coral Gables, Florida 33124
University of Michigan, Ann Arbor, Michigan 48109
University of Missouri–Columbia, Columbia, Missouri 65211
University of Nevada, Las Vegas, Nevada 89154
University of Oklahoma, Norman, Oklahoma 73019
University of Texas at El Paso, El Paso, Texas 79968
University of Utah, Salt Lake City, Utah 84112
University of Washington, Seattle, Washington, 98195
University of Wisconsin–Madison, Madison, Wisconsin 53706
University of Wyoming, Laramie, Wyoming 82071

Where Can I Get More Information About Meteorology?

For further information about careers in meteorology write to:

American Meteorological Society
45 Beacon Street
Boston, MA 02108

American Geophysical Union
1909 K Street, N.W.
Washington, DC 20006

For information about careers in the Federal government write to:

U.S. Civil Service Commission
1900 E Street, N.W.
Washington, DC 20250

National Oceanic and Atmospheric Administration
6001 Executive Boulevard
Rockville, MD 20852

OCEANOGRAPHY

The world is really one huge ocean, broken here and there by islands
that we call continents. To an outer space observer, our planet is blue.
Its name should be, perhaps, Oceanus, instead of earth. The oceans
cover over 140 million square miles of the earth's surface and reach
depths of more than six miles. All of the 92 natural elements can be
found in seawater, including millions of tons of gold and silver. The
ocean is filled with life. Plants grow along the shore and on the ocean's
surface. An amazing variety of animals, some microscopic and some
weighing several tons, are found in the sea. Some of the animals float
on the surface, some swim, and others live on the seafloor. The ocean
is never still. Its shoreline is constantly shifting, and its surface is forever
being ripped by waves. Currents flow beneath its surface, bringing warm
waters to Europe and cold, enriched nutrients to the fishing banks off
Labrador.

Oceanography is the study of the sea. *Oceanographers* are attempting
to understand and explain the processes within the ocean and the interrelationship between the ocean and the land and the ocean and the atmosphere. Oceanography involves the animals and plants that inhabit the
oceans, the minerals and fuels deposited within the seafloor, the weather
formed when the atmosphere meets the sea, the shoreline, the tides,
the beaches, the waves, and the sea currents. Oceanographic research
involves geology, meteorology, biology, chemistry, physics, geophysics,
geochemistry, fluid mechanics, and mathematics.

Many phases of marine research can be studied in the laboratory,
but to truly understand the ocean scientists must frequently go to sea
in specially constructed and equipped research ships. Sometimes data
regarding the shoreline, the beach, and the tides are obtained by oceanographers in a small dinghy; often, larger ships cruise the seas for months
with a crew of several oceanographers; and sometimes these scientists

go below the surface in scuba gear, diving suits, submarines, and, to reach the deepest regions, in bathyspheres.

The projects of oceanographers help in developing more accurate weather forecasts, breeding more fish for food, finding oil and minerals for economic and industrial growth, and aiding in the national defense.

What Do Oceanographers Do?

Some oceanographers work in laboratories associated with universities, where they study the minute details of animal and plant life found in the oceans. They may measure, dissect, and photograph fish. They may examine under high-powered microscopes the plankton, tiny plants and animals, that float on the surface of the oceans and serve as the major food source for most fish and sea animals, including the mammoth whales. These scientists are intrigued by identifying, cataloguing, and minutely observing the characteristics of the sea's living organisms.

Other oceanographers are interested in the mineral wealth of the seafloor. Using ultrasonic sonar, they probe the depths to locate likely regions where the sea has covered regions of prehistoric forests that have now turned to oil and natural gas. They map mountain ranges grander than the Rockies and gorges far deeper and wider than the Grand Canyon. If a possible resource is discovered, the oceanographer may suggest that extremely expensive drilling or mining begin.

Oceanographers explore and study the ocean from the surface, the beach, underwater, and from the air. The latest explorations are being carried out from satellites. They are charting the currents, the ocean depths, the temperature gradients, and the weather formed where the sea and atmosphere meet.

Oceanographers use specialized instruments to measure and record the findings of their explorations and studies. Special cameras equipped with strong lights are used to photograph marine life and the seafloor. Underwater seismometers record the echoes from underwater earthquakes and from depth charges ignited by scientists. Sonar units are used to detect schools of fish, underwater land formations, and submarines. Oceanographers want to know everything they can about the sea. They measure the salt content, which changes at various levels and in different bodies of water. They check on wave heights and the speed of currents. They want to know each and every kind of living species that inhabits the sea, and they want to understand the environmental factors that allow these plants and creatures survival.

Many phases of oceanography overlap, but there are a few occupations that can be distinguished. *Physical oceanography* is the study of the physical aspects of the ocean. *Physical oceanographers* study ocean currents, waves and tides, the chemical composition of seawater, and the sediments that fall to the bottom. Physical oceanographers work with meteorologists and geophysicists in trying to understand the processes of nature.

Chemical oceanographers investigate the chemical processes of the sea. The difference in salinity, salt content, between the Mediterranean Sea and the Atlantic Ocean allowed German U-boat commanders to slip past the sonar installations at Gibraltar by turning off their engines and allowing the osmotic force to propel them. Different kinds of marine life require different salt contents for survival, as well as different amounts of dissolved oxygen in the water. Undersea mining, oil wells, and global pollution have greatly affected the chemical content of seawater, which may cause the extinction of many species.

Geological oceanography is the study of the geological processes in the seafloor and along the shores. These marine geologists study the ocean's underwater mountain ranges, rocks, and sediments. Most are employed in trying to locate regions where oil, minerals, and natural gas might be found under the seafloor. One group of these scientists are working with plate tectonic geophysicists in studying and testing the theory of continental shift.

Biological oceanography is the study of the living creatures of the ocean. These scientists investigate the ecology, physiology, and taxonomy of plants and animals of the sea. Many marine biologists specialize in one group of creatures, such as sharks, mollusks, or sea worms. Some are working with agronomists to produce sea vegetation that can be harvested for human consumption. Others are trying to improve and control commercial fishing and to determine the effects of pollution on marine life.

Fishery is an applied branch of marine biology, which includes the problems of marketing, storing, and preparation of food fish. It is concerned with the biology of fishes, their population control, the changes that currents, tides, overfishing, and pollution have on the market value of fish. The industry is sometimes called aquaculture.

Many other scientists also work on problems related to oceans but are counted in other scientific fields such as biology, chemistry, or geology.

Where Are Oceanographers Employed?

There were only 2,700 persons working as oceanographers in 1976. It is one of the smallest of all scientific fields. This is rather surprising, considering the vastness and value of the oceans. However, neither the Federal government nor private industry wants to invest the capital required to develop the basic scientific understandings that will lead to a utilization of this resource.

About one-half of all oceanographers work as research and teaching faculty at colleges and universities. These professors spend about 50 percent of their time working with students, and the rest carrying out their investigations. Most of the universities that employ oceanographers are, of course, on either the Atlantic or Pacific Coast. A few, however, are inland.

The Federal government employs about one-fourth of all oceanographers. Many work for the National Oceanic and Atmospheric Administration or the Department of the Navy. The National Ocean Survey prepares charts and tables for navigation, for fishing, and for hydrographic studies. It has a fleet of research and survey ships that chart the coastal waters and tides.

The National Weather Service uses oceanographers to study the interaction between the atmosphere and the oceans, and to report on weather conditions at sea. The Environmental Research Laboratories of NOAA are carrying out basic research on the coastal environment, oceanic processes, the forces that produce severe storms and tsunamis, and so on. The National Fisheries Service seeks to develop the fishing industry in coastal waters and to protect the habitat of commercial and sport fish.

Some oceanographers work in private industry. They work for large shipping companies, for aquaculture corporations, and for mining and oil companies seeking fuel and minerals beneath the sea. State and local aquaria groups and a few private foundations, such as the International Oceanographic Foundation and The Cousteau Society, employ oceanographers to carry out basic research and to publicize and popularize the sea's important function in our global survival.

Most oceanographers work in states that border on the ocean, although there are some oceanographers in every state. Four out of ten oceanographers work in just three states—California, Maryland, and Virginia.

Oceanographers, whatever their special interest, are really sailor-scientists. They must go to sea for their information. Therefore, if you want to be an oceanographer, you should enjoy a life at sea. This may include days or weeks of tedious boredom, bad storms, repetitious recording of detailed data, seasickness, and long absences from the mainland. Many oceanographers are gathering information by making deep-sea dives in bathyspheres, submarines, and diving suits. Others use scuba outfits to investigate the water within 40 feet of the surface. Once the data is obtained, the oceanographers may spend months and years analyzing their findings at laboratories and computer centers back home.

How Can I Become an Oceanographer?

The minimum requirement for beginning professional jobs in oceanography is a bachelor's degree in oceanography, biology, geology, mathematics, or chemistry. However, most jobs in oceanography require graduate training, and a doctoral degree is often preferred or required.

There are very few openings for oceanographers, so the competition is keen. Only the most capable scientists will find jobs.

Oceanographers must be expert in mathematics, physics, geology, biology, and chemistry. To understand the oceans, the marine scientist must work with all the relationships in nature's physical-biological world. A biological oceanographer studying the habitat of a species of fish must investigate the chemistry of the seawater, the geology of the seafloor, the pressure exerted by the water above, the speed of the currents, the nature of the wave action, the temperature and light variations, as well as the anatomical structure of the creature, its activities, its sociology, its prey, and its predators.

In high school a future oceanographer must take chemistry, physics, and biology as well as any other science courses available. Oceanography is sometimes offered in secondary schools as an elective. Of course, this would be a good course, but do not take it instead of the major disciplines. Use it, along with subjects like photography and earth science, as extra preparation.

High school students who want to be oceanographers must obtain a solid background in mathematics. Take intermediate algebra, geometry, and trigonometry. If calculus is offered, it will make your advanced studies easier. Computer science is important in all fields of science; if a course is available at your school, you should take it, too.

Good English is essential. An oceanographer must be able to skillfully report his research to other scientists. You must be competent in English composition, have good sentence structure, and be able to express your ideas clearly and logically.

Jacques Cousteau, the most famous oceanographer, combined his interest in marine science and history to discover antiquities and sunken treasure ships at the bottom of the sea.

Since the oceans surround the globe and are vital for the commerce and defense of all nations of the world, the study of foreign languages is very useful to the oceanographer. French, Russian, Chinese, and Spanish are helpful and should be studied for two or more years in high school.

Only about 35 colleges offered undergraduate degrees in oceanography or marine science in 1976. However, a future oceanographer can receive a bachelor's degree in mathematics, physics, chemistry, geophysics, geology, meteorology, or biology and still anticipate acceptance in a graduate program in marine science. In fact, many graduate schools would prefer teaching the chemistry of seawater to a chemist, rather than trying to teach analytic chemistry to an oceanographer.

College students planning for careers in the marine sciences should acquire a strong undergraduate major in the basic sciences. The student should take courses in chemistry, physics, earth science or geology, and biology. Mathematics through calculus, statistics, and computer training are usually required for acceptance to a graduate program. Engineering courses and training in meteorology are very helpful. Of course, if you can major in oceanography as an undergraduate, that's terrific. However, make sure that you minor in one of the other sciences, so that you will have a broad background.

If your college does not offer coursework in oceanography, you may want to take introductory summer courses in marine science at a marine laboratory associated with a major university. Summer programs are offered at the University of Miami, Duke University, the University of Texas, Florida State University, Fairleigh Dickinson University, and the Marine Biological Laboratory at Woods Hole, Massachusetts.

In 1976 over 65 colleges offered graduate degrees in oceanography and marine sciences. Nineteen schools offer Ph.D degrees. The doctorate is required for most high-level research in the field. In graduate school the student receives advanced coursework. He or she trains under experts in the various specialized fields of oceanography. The student will often spend several months at sea, learning the techniques of the marine scientist. Only those who have very good academic credentials will be accepted to graduate programs in oceanography.

For the doctorate the candidate must write a dissertation on original research in oceanography. The doctoral student usually has to have mastered one or two foreign languages, as well as advanced mathematics, the physical and natural sciences, statistics, and computer programming.

The graduate program you might pick will depend on the areas of specialization that each school teaches. Some colleges specialize in fishery science or physical oceanography, whereas others offer broader ranges of studies.

What Are My Chances of Getting a Job as an Oceanographer?

In 1976 there were only 2,700 people working as oceanographers in the United States. The Federal government has predicted that by 1985 there will be a need for a total of about 4,000 oceanographers. Therefore, there will be only about 150 new jobs in oceanography every year. Most oceanographers are not near the age of retirement, so it is expected that there will be very few job openings, and the people hired will have exceptional credentials. Those with a Ph.D. degree should have a more favorable chance of finding employment in this field than others.

The jobs for oceanographers will be found at aquatic research stations, at state and Federal organizations, in industry, and at the science departments of universities and colleges. Many of the jobs are financed by grants from the Federal government; therefore if the government discovers the value of marine research, the job market may mushroom.

A few current projects that might increase the need for oceanographers are:

a) the mining of minerals, including iodine, magnesium, bromine, manganese, nickel, copper, and cobalt, from the sea.

b) the finding of oil and natural gas deposits in areas where drilling is profitable.

c) the harvesting of fish and seaweeds more profitably. Seaweed, incidentally, is now used in making medicine, candy, ice cream, jelly, salad dressing, and cosmetics.

d) the inexpensive desalting of seawater to make it fresh, so that it can be used as an irrigant and a water supply in desert countries.

e) the harnessing of the sea's energy to provide electricity.

f) the development of an inexpensive method for producing hydrogen from seawater. Hydrogen is an almost perfect fuel, whose waste product is water.

g) a global commitment to the elimination of pollution from the sea. As the world's population increases, it will need more and more resources, including food, from the oceans. If the sea continues to be a dumping ground for sewage and industrial, chemical, and radioactive wastes, mankind's life on earth is extremely limited.

These are a few areas in which rapid development could encourage the hiring of more trained oceanographers. However, you must be aware that each year many young people with training in marine science fail to find jobs. Those who get the jobs often have combined an interest in oceanography with experience and training in another scientific field or with engineering.

How Much Do Oceanographers Earn?

Oceanographers have relatively high salaries. In 1978 oceanographers in the Federal government with a bachelor's degree received starting salaries of around $11,000 a year. Those with a master's degree started at salaries up to $16,000, and those with a Ph.D. degree could earn up to $24,000. The average salary for experienced oceanographers in the Federal government in 1978 was about $26,000 a year. The salary for oceanographers employed by private industry may be as high as $30,000 a year.

Oceanographers who work at colleges and universities usually must have doctorates. They start at salaries around $16,000 an academic (nine-month) year and may rise to around $25,000. In addition to their salaries, many faculty members earn extra income from consulting, lecturing, and writing.

Oceanographers may be away from home for weeks or months at a time if they are engaged in research that involves sea voyages or trips to foreign countries. Sometimes they live and work in cramped quarters. They are subject to the perils of the sea, which may include severe storms and seasickness. People who like the sea and enjoy oceanographic research often find these voyages very satisfying and find this aspect of the job to be one of its real pleasures.

Where Can I Obtain Training in Oceanography?

Some of the colleges and universities that offer a major in oceanography are:

Alfred University, Alfred, New York 14802
Boston University, Boston, Massachusetts 02167
Bowdoin College, Brunswick, Maine 04011
University of Bridgeport, Bridgeport, Connecticut 06602
Catholic University, Washington, D.C. 20017
Clark University, Worcester, Massachusetts 01610
Columbia University, New York, N.Y. 10027
University of Connecticut, Storrs, Connecticut 06268
University of Delaware, Newark, Delaware 19711
Duke University, Durham, North Carolina 27706
Florida Institute of Technology, Melbourne, Florida 32901
Fordham University, New York, N.Y. 10458
Gulf Coast Junior College, Panama City, Florida 32401
Hope College, Holland, Michigan 49423
Johns Hopkins University, Baltimore, Maryland 21218
Lehigh University, Bethlehem, Pennsylvania 18015
Long Island University (C. W. Post Center), Greenvale, New York 11548
University of Maine, Orono, Maine 04473
Maritime College of the State University of New York, New York 10017
Miami-Dade Junior College, Miami, Florida 33139
S.U.N.Y. at Stony Brook, Stony Brook, New York 11790
New York University, New York, N.Y. 10003
University of North Carolina, Chapel Hill, North Carolina 27514
Northeastern University, Boston, Massachusetts 02115
Old Dominion University, Norfolk, Virginia 23508
University of the Pacific, Stockton, California 95204
University of Rhode Island, Kingston, Rhode Island 02881
Rutgers State University of New Jersey, New Brunswick, New Jersey 08903
Rensselaer Polytechnic Institute, Troy, New York 12181
San Jose State College, San Jose, California 95114
Southeastern Massachusetts University, North Dartmouth, Massachusetts 02747
St. John's University, New York, N.Y. 11432
Suffolk University, Boston, Massachusetts 02167
Texas A & M University, College Station, Texas 77840
Tufts College, Medford, Massachusetts 02155
Washington and Lee University, Lexington, Virginia 24450
Webb Institute of Naval Architecture, Glen Cove, New York 11542
University of Wisconsin, Madison, Wisconsin 53706
Woods Hole Oceanographic Institution, Woods Hole, Massachusetts 02543

Where Can I Get More Information About Oceanography?

For further information on careers in oceanography write to:

The U.S. Department of Commerce
National Oceanic and Atmospheric Administration
6001 Executive Boulevard
Rockville, MD 20852

International Oceanographic Foundation
3979 Rickenbacker Causeway
Virginia Key, Miami, FL 33149

For detailed information about oceanography read:

Your Future in the Science of Oceanography by Jonathan S. Wood. Richards Rosen Press.

Chapter IX

Conservation Sciences: Forestry, Range Management, Soil Conservation

CONSERVATION SCIENCE

Conservation is the protection and wise management of the environment. Scientists and concerned citizens practice conservation so that the environment can continue to provide for the needs of living things. Without conservation, all the resources necessary for life—air, animals, energy, minerals, plants, soil, and water—would be damaged, wasted, or destroyed.

Conservation also involves a concern for the quality of the environment so that people can enjoy living. It means keeping the environment comfortable and safe. A healthy environment contains cities that are free of junk and litter, air and water that are uncontaminated, parks that provide green space for the community, and wilderness regions where animals and plants can be safe from destruction.

It was once thought that the earth's resources were unlimited. Cities and industries thought that the rivers and oceans could consume all the wastes they could manufacture. Forestry companies thought that they could cut down all the trees, farmers thought that they could overwork the soil, hunters and trappers overkilled wildlife, and the "modernized" nations assumed that they could increasingly consume fuel. It is now apparent that people must learn to use the earth's resources much more wisely. If they do not, life may perish.

It is the responsibility of *conservation scientists* to help the governments, industries, and citizens of the world to understand the safeguards needed to protect the environment. Conservation scientists monitor the earth's resources, develop methods for their protection, and help manage them to assure that future needs will be met.

Conservation scientists are concerned with soil, water, air, forests,

117

wildlife, grazing land, minerals and fuels, recreation areas, and the urban environment. Each type of conservation has its own problems and solutions, but all are related. Many occupations in the sciences involve conservation. Oceanographers are concerned with pollution of the oceans. Meteorologists are studying ways to clean the air. Biologists and medical scientists are investigating the effects of an uncontrolled industrial society on plants, animals, and man. Geologists are trying to isolate the factors that contribute to a good watershed so that fresh water can be maintained. Statisticians and mathematicians are trying to describe the parameters that can be controlled so that industrial growth can continue without destroying a resource. Chemists are developing methods for reclaiming wasted regions and for manufacturing goods that are less harmful. The list goes on and on.

Many of the scientists who work on conservation problems were trained in a traditional domain such as chemistry, life science, physics, or geology. There are some conservation occupations, however, that usually require specialized training for admission. In this chapter we shall look at three of those occupations: forester, range manager, and soil conservationist.

What Do Conservation Scientists Do?

Our forests are a vital natural resource. They slow the runoff of rain, which provides fresh water and checks erosion. They provide homes for wildlife and offer opportunities for recreation. They provide timber for the paper, chemical, home furnishings, and construction industries. Rayon is made from material from wood as are thousands of other useful products. Well-managed forests supply our world in many ways and provide jobs for workers in the forest-products industry.

Forests can be destroyed, too, in many ways. Trees can be cut down without new ones being planted. Forest fires can be caused by lightning or by accident. Insects and plant diseases have damaged many forests. If a forest is lost, it may take generations before it can be restored. Well-protected forests, however, can serve man indefinitely. Unlike our mineral reserves, they are a renewable resource.

Foresters are the scientists responsible for managing, developing, and protecting these lands and their resources—timber, water, wildlife, forage, and recreational areas. They may plan and supervise the cutting and planting of trees. They may study how trees grow and try to protect them from fire, harmful insects, and disease. They may supervise camps, parks, and grazing lands. They may do research, help forestry industries, or teach the public about the forests and how they can be conserved.

Forestry deals with the management of forests and forest lands so that they can provide a continuous production of goods and services. Most jobs in forestry are concerned with the management of land. An industrially owned tract may be managed by foresters for the production of timber crops for lumber, pulp and paper, or other wood products. A tract of watershed land owned by a city, state, or the Federal government, or by a water company will be managed primarily to improve and protect its values as a source of fresh water. National and State Parks are established for their scenic values and to facilitate public study and enjoyment. Foresters who work in parks help to maintain their beauty and try to ensure that they are used properly. On a wildlife refuge, a forester may want to keep the public away so that a proper habitat can be maintained.

Even on a single-purpose area, foresters have a variety of responsibilities. They may have to make land surveys or supervise the cutting and planting of trees. They may need to plan and direct the reforestation of some cut-over or burned-over lands or conduct special soil erosion control or flood control measures. They also must plan and direct the control of forest fires and tree pests such as insects.

Foresters also do research. They may study ways to control certain forest insects, or they may be interested in the watershed management in a mountain snow zone, or they may want to improve nursery and planting methods.

Some provide forestry information to the general public and to forest owners. Courses are taught by foresters at many colleges and universities.

Foresters often specialize in one area of work, such as timber management, outdoor recreation, or forest economics. Sometimes, if a forester has acquired considerable expertise in one area, he or she might become a private consultant. Private forestry consultants are hired by large companies and by the Federal or state governments to help solve a particular problem.

Forestry technicians, sometimes called forestry aides, assist foresters in the care and management of forest lands and their resources. These nonprofessional workers may cruise timber, look out for fires, scale logs, assist in surveys, or guard forest areas. Technicians work on many forest improvement projects. They inspect trees for disease and other problems and record their findings. They work to prevent flood damage and soil erosion and seek ways to increase the quality of water in the forest. Technicians may maintain forest areas for hunting, camping, hiking, and other recreational activities. They may aid in the planting of new trees after a fire or a major harvest.

Rangelands cover more than one billion acres of the United States, mostly in the Western states and Alaska. They contain many natural resources: grass and shrubs for animal grazing, habitats for livestock and wildlife, water from vast watersheds, facilities for water sports and other kinds of recreation, and valuable mineral and energy resources. *Range managers* manage, improve, and protect range resources.

Range managers are sometimes called range scientists, range ecologists, or range conservationists. Many range managers work for livestock ranches. They plan ways to effectively and economically use the range-lands. A range manager might determine the kind and number of animal most suited for grazing on a particular land area. After grazing, the range manager may have to reseed the area or remove brush to keep it fertile. A range conservationist is particularly aware of the balance that must be maintained between profitable grazing by herds and the needs of wildlife.

Range managers study the rangelands and try to improve them by such techniques as controlled burning, reseeding, and control of insect pests and undesirable plants. They are often responsible, too, for providing for animal watering facilities, erosion control, and fire prevention. Range managers may also be involved in protecting and controlling timber lands, as well as outdoor recreational facilities.

Both range managers and foresters are involved in watershed management. This involves the establishment of erosion controls by planting shrubs and trees, disallowing uncontrolled timber harvests and overgrazing, and developing drainage and dam systems. The maintaining of fresh water supplies is very important to the farmer and to every citizen. Many conservation scientists work full time in protecting this resource.

Soil conservationists provide technical assistance to farmers, ranchers, and others concerned with the proper use of one of the earth's most precious resources. Only three-tenths of the earth's surface is land; the rest is covered with water. Much of the land is too cold, too hot, too mountainous, or too wet for growing crops. As a result, less than 1 acre of land per human on the earth is arable, that is, suitable for farming. Soil conservationists are the experts who know how to develop the land so that it can produce a maximum yield for a long period of time.

Soil conservationists help farmers and other land managers develop programs that make the most productive use of land without damaging it. They do most of their work in the field. If a farmer is having trouble with erosion, the soil conservationist will examine the land and analyze the soil. The conservationist may suggest terracing the land or may develop a system of runoffs that will prevent too much water from soaking into the soil. Better farming methods might be suggested, or, if wind is blowing the topsoil away, hedges might be recommended as windbreaks.

The soil conservationist works with agronomists and chemists in developing fertilizers that will enrich the soil and allow continuous planting. The conservationist works with hydrologists and engineers in developing better irrigation techniques.

The conservationist works with range managers in analyzing areas where overgrazing has occurred or where fresh water is running low. Close attention is paid to weather patterns. Excessive snowfall or an early spring might cause flooding that could damage thousands of acres unless precautionary measures are taken. Similarly, droughts may require unusual methods to save a harvest. The soil conservationist must be expert in many fields, in order to work most effectively.

All the conservation careers involve work in the outdoors. Some require considerable time spent in rugged remote areas. In emergencies, such as fighting fires and controlling floods, conservationists must work many extra hours. Sometimes the work is hazardous, but often it can be very routine. Long stretches of monotonous testing, marking, or observing at an isolated outpost may be required. Sometimes a considerable amount of paperwork must be processed in a downtown office.

Conservationists should be able to write and speak effectively, since much of their work is based on convincing others that careful conservation is reason enough to forego the profit which can be gained from an area. They should be able to work alone and have the ability to make decisions. Many jobs require good physical health and stamina, but opportunities are available for the handicapped to work in these vital fields.

Where Are Conservationists Employed?

About 30,000 persons worked as foresters in 1979. About 10,000 worked in private industry. Most of the work in the private sector was for pulp and paper, lumber, logging, and milling companies. Nearly 6,000 foresters worked for the Federal government, primarily in the Forest Service of the Department of Agriculture. The remainder worked for state and local governments, colleges, and universities. Some were self-employed, either as consultants or forest owners. In addition, 11,000 people were employed in 1976 as forestry technicians.

The work of a forester in a state forest or an industrial forest is generally similar, except that in an industrial forest a greater proportion of the work would probably be devoted to the growing and harvesting of the timber. Both would involve timber inventory, harvest planning, seeding or planting, fire and pest prevention, and so on.

Forestry usually involves working in a rural or, sometimes, isolated area. A new occupation, however, called urban forestry involves working for a city or county to develop and maintain tree programs in heavily populated areas.

Research in forestry is carried on by the U.S. Forest Service, by some state agencies, by colleges and universities, and by some larger forest industry companies. The Forest Service, in the U.S. Department of Agriculture, carries out the most comprehensive research program. It maintains ten regional research units. Within each of the regions, the Forest Service maintains a number of project centers and experimental forests. The headquarters of the Forest Service are in Washington, D.C., and the world's largest institution devoted to the study of wood is at the Forest Products Laboratory in Madison, Wisconsin. This facility, run in cooperation with the University of Wisconsin, conducts research designed to increase the usefulness of forest products. The Forest Service studies a different kind of forest at its Institute of Tropical Forestry in Puerto Rico.

Some foresters work for trade associations of pulp and paper manufacturers, lumbermen, and other forestry groups. Others work for organizations that are primarily interested in conservation, such as the American Forestry Association. Many work as teachers. Some work for banks and industrial firms that need information about forests, and many work with engineers in planning roads and construction in forest areas.

About 3,000 persons worked as range managers in 1976. Most worked for the Federal government. The Forest Service and the Soil Conservation Service of the Department of Agriculture are the principal employers. The Bureau of Land Management of the Department of the Interior also hires some range managers. Range managers in state governments are usually employed in game and fish departments, state land agencies, and extension services.

An increasing number of range managers are finding work for private companies. Some are employed by livestock and agribusiness concerns. Coal and oil companies are hiring range managers to help restore the ecological balance that was disturbed by open-pit mining and other destructive drilling and mining techniques. Banks and real estate firms employ them to help develop the value of range areas.

Some range managers with advanced degrees teach and do research at colleges and universities. A few find employment with hunting clubs, conservation organizations, and other public and private agencies concerned about developing and protecting the range. Many people who study range conservation plan to manage their own livestock ranches. Most range managers work in the Western states and in Alaska.

Approximately 7,500 soil conservationists were employed in 1976. Most worked for the Soil Conservation Service of the U.S. Department of Agriculture. Some worked for the Department of the Interior's Bureau of Indian Affairs. Many soil conservationists for the Federal government work as advisers for Soil and Water Conservation Districts in almost every county in the country. Those employed by the Bureau of Indian Affairs generally work near or on Indian reservations, most of which are in the Western states. Soil conservationists work for state and local governments, and some teach at colleges and universities.

The Soil Conservation Service is the country's leading employer of soil conservationists. It sends out experts to help farmers and ranchers improve their lands. It also aids watershed groups, recreation agencies, construction and highway developers, and those concerned with irrigation. The Soil Conservation Service also employs agronomists, soil scientists, foresters, range conservationists, engineers, biologists, geologists, hydrologists, and agricultural economists.

Some soil conservationists are employed by rural banks, insurance firms, and mortgage companies that make loans for agricultural lands.

A few work for lumber and paper companies, agribusiness industries, and other concerns that have large holdings of forested lands. Public utilities such as water companies employ soil conservationists to study and improve their watershed properties.

How Can I Become a Conservationist?

A bachelor's degree with a major in forestry is the minimum educational requirement for a job as a forester. However, because there are more people receiving forestry degrees than there are jobs, most employers prefer candidates who also hold advanced degrees. Jobs as teachers and those in research require a master's degree or a Ph.D.

In 1976 some 50 colleges and universities offered bachelor's degrees in forestry; 43 of these were accredited by the Society of American Foresters. During the first two years, forestry students generally build a strong background in science, engineering, mathematics, economics, and social studies. In the junior and senior years they take technical courses in forestry. Most programs also include courses in forest economics and business administration. Many colleges require students to spend one summer in a field camp, where they receive "in-the-woods" training. Many students get summer jobs with the U.S. Forest Service, where they receive firsthand experience in forest conservation work.

Although college is generally not a required condition for a job as a forestry technician, the keen job competition favors those with some junior college training. In 1976 about 80 technical institutes, junior or community colleges, and universities offered forestry technician training; 53 of these institutions were recognized by the Society of American Foresters. At these schools, students receive general academic coursework, including biology, mathematics, and botany, and forest technology courses such as land surveying, tree identification, aerial photograph interpretation, and timber harvesting. In addition, forestry technicians usually spend a summer at a forest or camp learning specialized techniques firsthand.

For jobs as range managers, the usual requirement is a bachelor's degree in range management or range science. Sometimes a degree in agronomy or forestry, with coursework in range management, is acceptable. Research and college teaching positions usually require a graduate degree. In 1976 about 20 colleges and universities had degree programs in range science. A number of other schools offered some coursework in the field.

Training in range management requires a basic knowledge of biology, chemistry, physics, and mathematics. Specialized courses are taken in plant, animal, and soil sciences. Range scientists study ecology, economics, and forestry as well as economics, wildlife management, and recreation administration. Some colleges offer summer camp courses on the range, and many range managers get summer jobs with the Federal government to learn their specialty.

Very few colleges and universities offer a specific degree in soil conservation. Most soil conservationists receive bachelor's degrees in agronomy, the science of soil and crop management. A few soil conservationists have degrees in related fields of forestry, agriculture, biology, and so on. In college you should take courses in agricultural engineering, cartography (mapmaking), agricultural sciences, chemistry, biology, physics, English, and the communications arts. Of course, special training in soil chemistry is important. Advanced graduate training is required for jobs in teaching and research.

In high school prospective conservationists should take a college preparatory program. You should take all the sciences, especially chemistry and biology. It is not necessary, or perhaps even desirable, to specialize in conservation-related subjects. You will learn all you need to know in college. If you can take physics, that is preferable to an ecology or earth science class. Take as much mathematics as you can handle, and also develop your communications skills, such as writing and speaking. Conservationists must communicate well with people, since their work deals with educating farmers, ranchers, politicians, industrialists, journalists, and the public in sound conservation practices. Also, they must be able to prepare written reports and plans of programs to present to organizations and local and national government agencies.

Conservationists usually begin their careers under the supervision of experienced scientists. After gaining skills, they may advance to more responsible positions. An experienced conservationist may supervise an entire forest or range or a state's total environmental program. In private industry conservationists start by learning the practical and administrative aspects of the business. Many conservation scientists work their way up to top managerial positions within their companies.

What Are My Chances of Getting a Job as a Conservation Scientist?

In 1979 about 30,000 persons worked as foresters in the United States. Over the next decade, there will be about 1,000 new jobs a year in this field. Currently, many more than 1,000 students each year graduate with degrees in forestry. Therefore, there is stiff competition for jobs. Opportunities will be better for those who have an advanced degree, specialized training, or several years' experience.

There may be an increase in job opportunities, however, as private owners of timberland may find an increasingly profitable market for forest products and forest services. Wood is a renewable energy resource. Some research has indicated that cottonwood forests might be able to compete with oil or coal as a fuel resource. If this trend develops, it could produce many jobs for professionals in the field. An increasing awareness by the public and private sector of environmental protection may also stimulate jobs for foresters.

About 12,000 persons worked full time as forestry technicians in 1979. Over the next decade about 500 new jobs a year should develop. In addition, there were about 11,000 temporary jobs, primarily with the Federal and state governments, during the summer and in the spring and fall seasons. Nearly half the year-round total worked in private industry. There may be a rapid increase in the employment of forestry technicians, since they can perform many of the routine tasks now carried out by more highly paid professional foresters. This will allow the forester more time to devote to supervisory work and to the general management of the forest.

In 1976 there were about 3,000 range managers in the United States. By 1985, the Department of Labor predicts, about 4,000 will be needed. Percentagewise, this is an incredible increase. However, it only means about 100 new jobs a year. Job opportunities are expected to be good for persons with degrees in range management or range science.

Since the amount of rangeland is generally fixed, range managers will be needed to increase the output of rangelands while protecting their ecology. Cattle are spending less time on the range being fattened for slaughter; this may limit the growth of livestock herds and make finding a job as a range manager more difficult. However, legislation regarding wildlife protection and the requirements placed on mining companies to restore the ecological balance they upset should create an additional need.

About 7,500 soil conservationists were employed in 1976. Each year there should be new jobs for a few hundred. The Department of Agriculture is especially interested in this new field and each year is increasing the number of soil conservationists it hires.

Banks, public utilities, and other organizations that make loans on agricultural lands will continue to hire more of these specialists to evaluate their properties, make them more profitable, and help them comply with recent conservation and antipollution laws. As concern for the environment and an interest in land development grows, a larger number of colleges may add soil conservation programs to their curricula. This would increase the demand for teachers of soil conservation.

The conservation fields are very attractive, and many people are majoring in them in college. The competition is very high for any interesting job. Many people with degrees in forestry, soil conservation, and range science cannot find work directly in their fields. Successful applicants often have special skills, training, advanced degrees, or experience.

How Much Do Conservation Scientists Earn?

In 1978 the average starting salary for a forester with a bachelor's degree was close to $12,000; for those with a master's degree the starting salary was close to $14,000. Experienced foresters earned an average salary over $20,000 in 1978. Some forest products experts earn salaries over $35,000 a year.

There are over 25,000 people employed as foresters in the U.S. The Federal government has about 6,000 on its payroll. The average forester for the Federal government in 1979 earned $23,922 a year. The starting salary in 1979 for those with a bachelor's degree and no experience was $11,243. However, because of keen competition, most foresters hired by the Federal government held a master's degree or had some experience, and generally started at $13,925 or $17,035. Foresters with a Ph.D. started at $20,611 or $24,703, depending on experience and specialized training.

In local government foresters generally earn slightly less than those working for the Federal government. Salaries for foresters working for colleges and universities in 1979 averaged around $25,000 for those with a doctorate. Starting salaries were close to $18,000 for universities and around $15,000 for two-year colleges. Many foresters supplement their salaries with income from lecturing, consulting, and writing.

Starting salaries for forestry technicians ranged from $9,000 to $12,000 in 1979. Experienced forestry technicians earned an average salary over $18,000. In the Federal government in 1979 forestry technicians could start at $10,000 to $11,000 a year, depending on education and experience. Experienced forestry technicians with the Federal government could earn around $17,000 a year in 1979. Many forestry technician jobs are not full-year employment. Climatic conditions, such as snow cover in the winter, cause seasonal layoffs. Extra hours, with extra pay, are often available during emergencies such as floods and forest fires.

The pay scales for soil and range conservationists are similar to those for foresters. In the Federal government in 1979 there were 4,490 soil conservationists, whose average salary was $22,072. There were 1,094 range conservationists, whose average salary was $19,168. Starting salaries are identical to those for foresters.

Where Can I Obtain Training in the Conservation Sciences?

Some of the colleges and universities that offer majors in conservation science are:

> Abilene Christian College, Abilene, Texas 79601
> University of Arizona, Tucson, Arizona 85721
> Bradley University, Peoria, Illinois 61606
> Brevard College, Brevard, North Carolina 28712
> Central Michigan University, Mount Pleasant, Michigan 48858
> University of Connecticut, Storrs, Connecticut 06268
> Douglas College of Rutgers University, New Brunswick, New Jersey 08903
> Duke University, Durham, North Carolina 27706

University of Florida, Gainesville, Florida 32611
University of Idaho, Moscow, Idaho 83843
Kansas State University, Manhattan, Kansas 66502
Kent State University, Kent, Ohio 44242
Louisiana Tech University, Ruston, Louisiana 71270
University of Maine, Orono, Maine 04473
Miami University, Oxford, Ohio 45056
Michigan State University, East Lansing, Michigan 48824
University of Minnesota, Minneapolis, Minnesota 55455
Murray State University, Murray, Kentucky 42071
University of Nevada, Reno, Nevada 89507
University of New Hampshire, Durham, New Hampshire 03824
New Mexico State University, Las Cruces, New Mexico 88003
North Carolina State University, Raleigh, North Carolina 27607
Ohio State University, Columbus, Ohio 43212
Purdue University, Lafayette, Calumet, North Central Campuses, West
    Lafayette, Hammond, Westville, Indiana
Rutgers University, New Brunswick, New Jersey 08903
Southern Illinois University, Edwardsville, Illinois 62025
State University of New York Agricultural and Technical College, Cobles-
    kill, New York 12043
State University of New York College of Agriculture at Cornell University,
    Ithaca, New York 14850
State University of New York College of Forestry, Syracuse, New York
    13210
Texas Tech University, Lubbock, Texas 79409
Utah State University, Logan, Utah 84322
University of Vermont, Burlington, Vermont 05401
Weber State College, Ogden, Utah 84403
West Virginia University, Morgantown, West Virginia 26506
University of Wyoming, Laramie, Wyoming 82070

Some of the colleges and universities that offer a major in forestry
are:

Auburn University, Auburn, Alabama 36830
University of California, Berkeley, California 94720
Clemson University, Clemson, South Carolina 29631
Colorado State University, Fort Collins, Colorado 80521
University of Florida, Gainesville, Florida 32611
University of Georgia, Athens, Georgia 30602
University of Idaho, Moscow, Idaho 83843
Iowa State University, Ames, Iowa 50010
University of Maine, Orono, Maine 04473
Michigan State University, East Lansing, Michigan 48824
Michigan Technological University, Houghton, Michigan 49931
Mississippi State University, State College, Mississippi 39762
University of Montana, Missoula, Montana 59801

University of New Hampshire, Durham, New Hampshire 03824
North Carolina State University, Raleigh, North Carolina 27607
Northern Arizona University, Flagstaff, Arizona 86001
Oregon State University, Corvallis, Oregon 97331
Pennsylvania State University, University Park, Pennsylvania 16802
Purdue University, Lafayette, Calumet and North Central Campuses, West
    Lafayette, Hammond, and Westville, Indiana
State University of Environmental Science and Forestry, Syracuse, New
    York 13210
University of Tennessee, Knoxville, Tennessee 37916
University of Vermont, Burlington, Vermont 05401
Virginia Polytechnical Institute, Blacksburg, Virginia 24061
Washington State University, Pullman, Washington 99163
West Virginia University, Morgantown, West Virginia 26506
University of Wisconsin, Madison, Wisconsin 53706

Where Can I Get More Information About the Conservation Sciences?

For further information on careers in conservation write to:

Fish and Wildlife Service
U.S. Department of the Interior
Washington, DC 20240

National Wildlife Federation
1412 16th Street N.W.
Washington, DC 20036

Wildlife Management Institute
709 Wire Building
Washington, DC 20005

American Forestry Association
1319 18th Street N.W.
Washington, DC 20036

American Forest Institute
1619 Massachusetts Avenue N.W.
Washington, DC 20036

Society of American Foresters
1010 16th Street N.W.
Washington, DC 20036

U.S. Forest Service
Department of Agriculture
1621 North Kent Street
Arlington, VA 20415

American Society of Range Management
2120 South Birch Street
Denver, CO 80222

American Society of Agronomy
677 South Segoe Road
Madison, WI 53711

Soil Conservation Society of America
7515 Northeast Ankeny Road
Ankeny, IA 50021

For detailed information about a career in forestry read:

Your Future in Forestry by David Hanaburgh, Richards Rosen Press, Inc.

Chapter X

The Mathematical Sciences: Classical Mathematics, Statistics, Computer Science

MATHEMATICS

Mathematics is central to understanding nature. Physicists and astronomers rely on precise measurements, which are analyzed for their mathematical relationships. An early physicist-mathematician, Archimedes, found that there was a mathematical relationship between mass and volume that is an identifying characteristic of a substance. This relationship is called specific gravity. With this knowledge, Archimedes proved that a jeweler had cheated the king by substituting another material for gold within a crown he had manufactured. The jeweler lost his head, and science triumphed.

Today, advanced mathematics is providing an understanding of the basic forces of the universe that govern the stars and the particles within an atom. In the life sciences, statistics plays an important role in interpreting the variety found among living creatures. Except for clones, which are common in horticulture, no two organisms are identical. Even identical twins respond differently to light, heat, radiation, chemicals, and so on. If a new pesticide is sprayed on a field of grain to eliminate a species of insect, 99.9999 percent of that pest may succumb to the drug. However, the 0.0001 percent that survive can pass on to their offspring their immunity to the drug. This may produce, within a growing season, an insect variety that is immune to the pesticide and can continue to devastate the crop.

Chemical and biochemical reactions are mathematically analyzed to determine how molecules and atoms interact to form new compounds that can be beneficial. The greatest chemists of this century, people like Niels Bohr, Linus C. Pauling, Erwin Schrödinger, James D. Watson, and Francis H. C. Crick, received their Nobel prizes for achievements in applying advanced mathematical techniques to describe the structure of nature.

The basis of modern chemistry is the Schrödinger equation, which describes the wave and particle properties of the simplest atom in the universe, hydrogen. In its one-dimensional form, the Schrödinger equation is:

$$\frac{\partial^2 \psi}{\partial x^2} + \frac{8\pi^2 M}{h^2}(E - P)\psi = 0$$

x stands for one dimension; h = a constant, 6.626×10^{-27} erg-sec; m = the mass of the particle; E = the total energy of the particle, which is the sum of its kinetic and potential energy; P = the potential energy of the particle; and the Greek letter psi, ψ = the distribution of the electron. ∂ is a function (such as +, −, ×, etc.) in calculus. This still does not completely describe the system of only one electron and one proton.

After Schrödinger announced his work in 1926, other scientists found that newer mathematical theories were needed. Paul Dirac invented a form of matrix algebra to handle the work. Today, chemists work with mathematicians to find order in the macromolecules of proteins, carbohydrates, and nucleic acids, which are 20,000 times heavier and billions of times more complex than hydrogen.

Mathematics is the oldest and most vital of all sciences. Mathematicians today are engaged in a wide variety of activities, ranging from the creation of new theories to the translation of scientific and managerial problems into mathematical terms. Their tools are the pencil and the computer. They take a vast array of facts and manipulate them to come up with simpler, comprehensible formulas. With the power of the computer at their command, mathematicians can take such various facts as age, sex, geographical location, smoking habits, family background, occupation, education, and diet and derive consistent theories regarding life span, health, and mental hygiene of the members of a group. Mathematicians are involved in predicting the growth of the country's economy, its consumption of fuels, its buying habits, and so on.

Mathematical work falls into two broad classes: *theoretical* (pure) *mathematics* and *applied mathematics.* However, these classes are not sharply defined and often overlap.

Theoretical mathematicians often deal with pure numbers. They advance the mathematical sciences by developing new principles and by discovering new relationships between existing theories. Their work, which is often so abstract that it no longer deals with the physical dimensions of the universe, increases our basic knowledge. Although the work of *pure mathematicians* usually develops along purely mental pathways, it has often led the way to discovering new concepts that have produced many scientific and engineering achievements.

Mathematicians in applied work use mathematics to solve practical problems in business, government, engineering, and the natural and social sciences. Their work includes the problems of sending a manned spaceship to the moon, the effects of new drugs on disease, the most efficient method of shipping merchandise from a factory to stores, the design of a fuselage that will have less wind resistance, and the structure of a prehistoric creature from bone fragments.

What Do Mathematicians Do?

The role of the mathematician is varied. Many are teachers, some work in industry, others for the government. There are mathematicians who are specialists in computer science and others who work as statisticians. Mathematicians who work for the U.S. Navy use their training differently from those who work for banks. Let us look at some of the occupations for mathematicians.

Computer mathematicians, who are sometimes called *systems programmers, systems engineers,* or *systems analysts,* are the experts who know how to talk to the computer. Almost every industry in the world now makes extensive use of computers. There is a great demand for people who can evaluate the problems and needs of a company, translate them into computer language, and let the computer help to find the best solution.

Computer mathematicians figure out how a computer can monitor a nuclear powerplant, route thousands of telephone calls instantaneously, and forecast sales for a manufacturer of refrigerators. Some computer mathematicians improve systems already in use; others do research in devising new methods that are quicker, simpler, and cheaper.

Operations researchers, who are sometimes called *operations analysts* or the ambiguous *systems analysts,* are highly trained mathematicians who try to interpret complicated economic and business problems. An operations researcher for a construction firm might try to develop a computer model that can predict the housing needs of a community for the next twenty years. This would require the manipulation of statistics regarding family growth, jobs, highways, recreational sources, energy requirements, and sewage and waste disposal. The real world is very complex. Events such as global disharmony or the invention of a vehicle that can go five hundred miles on a gallon of alcohol can seriously alter the best predictions, but large companies and governments must have the best information available for their long-term, far-reaching concerns.

Statisticians devise, carry out, and interpret the numerical results of surveys and experiments. The Nielsen Rating and the Harris Election Polls are examples of surveys carried out by statisticians, who obtain accurate information about large groups of people by surveying only

A minicomputer displays graphs of several variables of an economic model.

a small portion, called a sample. In the Nielsen Television Rating, for example, only a few thousand families are used to determine how many of a family audience of fifty million are watching a particular show. The Harris Polls showed the power of well-planned critical sampling when they predicted that Harry S. Truman would win the Presidency in 1948, despite the overwhelming press consensus that he would lose.

Biostatisticians often work for drug, cosmetic, and food companies, where they set up statistical tests for new products to determine if they are safe for human use. Sometimes their results indicate that the overall effects are good and safe but that certain groups, such as pregnant women or diabetics, should avoid the product.

Statistics is used in all of the sciences. Boltzmann-Einstein statistics, for example, has developed into a powerful tool for helping chemists understand chemical reactions. Economists use statistics to help explain why certain government programs are needed to stimulate the economy or why certain programs failed in their mission. Statistics is a meaningful way to report a vast array of data. Decision-makers need statisticians to help them extract what is important and what is reliable, so that they can use the information effectively.

The *information mathematician* or *scientist* is concerned with the sending and storage of, simply, information. The communications industry uses information scientists to help them develop the electromagnetic theories that allow words to be changed to electrical signals suitable for transmission over telephone cables, FM or AM radio broadcasts, satellite relays, and television microwaves. Other titles for information scientists are *control system scientists, signal processors,* or *communications systems scientists* or *analysts.*

Many information scientists work for computer companies, where they design systems for storing and retrieving data. These systems are used for maintaining business records, accounts, scientific information, census data, automatic libraries, and tax information. The speed with which data can be entered, compiled with other information, and recovered is constantly improving. "Data banks" containing such information as the credit status of most Americans, the location of people with rare blood types, the occurrence of serious diseases, and the addresses of people who like mail-order merchandise are used every day.

Other applications of information science are in the analysis of geophysical records to locate petroleum deposits or the organization of displays and communications in air traffic control systems. Information scientists help design thermostats that control the temperature of rooms, complex aircraft autopilots, sophisticated control systems for automated factories and powerplants, and guidance systems for space exploration vehicles.

Classical mathematicians are the ones who work with abstract number theory. They are mainly employed in colleges and universities. Some, however, work for private industry or for the Federal government. They may be interested in either pure or applied mathematics. They are often concerned with the same kinds of problems that interest physicists. They want to achieve a basic understanding of the forces of the universe. In fact, most astrophysicists (astronomers), atomic and subatomic physicists, and nuclear physicists are actually mathematicians. The stars and the particles they are interested in cannot be manipulated in the laboratory, so they must rely on mathematics to perform the experiments necessary for scientific discovery. Classical applied mathematicians are interested in the stability of structures, the propagation of electromagnetic waves (television, radio, ultraviolet, light, heat, X-rays) and other physically oriented areas. The pure mathematicians search for solutions to difficult theoretical problems. Many have applied their talents to devising new techniques for solving difficult problems with the computer. Equations that would have taken hundreds of years to solve by hand can be solved in a few minutes with today's technology.

Where Are Mathematicians Employed?

About half of all mathematical specialists are teachers by profession. They teach in secondary schools, community colleges, four-year colleges, and universities. Many combine their teaching with research and development in mathematics.

About three-fourths of the 38,000 classical mathematicians work in colleges and universities. The others have found interesting jobs, usually in applied mathematics, for the aerospace, communications, electronics, and mechanical industries. The Department of Defense and the National Aeronautics and Space Administration employed most of the 5,268 mathematicians working in the Federal government in 1979.

Classical mathematicians who teach work in all states. Those who work in industry and those who are employed by large colleges and universities must work near big cities. Nearly half of the classical mathematicians are employed in seven states—California, New York, Massachusetts, Pennsylvania, Illinois, Maryland, and New Jersey. One-fourth of all mathematicians live in only three metropolitan areas—New York City, Washington, D.C., and Los Angeles.

Almost 200,000 persons worked as computer specialists and operations researchers in 1980. Many worked for manufacturing firms, banks, insurance companies, and data processing services. Large numbers worked for wholesale and retail businesses and for the government. In 1979 over 60,000 computer specialists worked for the Federal government. The U.S. Department of Commerce employs computer mathematicians to aid the National Oceanic and Atmospheric Administration in its weather prediction service and its environmental surveys.

All branches of the government use experts in the use of computers. The Census Bureau, the Federal Bureau of Investigation, the Internal Revenue Service, the Defense Department, the National Aeronautics and Space Administration, and the National Institutes of Health have extensive computer facilities that are monitored and improved by highly trained mathematicians.

More than one-third of all computer mathematicians and operations researchers are employed in the Midwest, and about one-fourth work in the Northeast.

In 1976 approximately 24,000 persons worked as statisticians. About two-thirds worked in private industry. They worked with market research staffs of manufacturers, banks and insurance companies, and for public utilities. About 3,000 worked for the Federal government in 1979. In the Department of Commerce statisticians gather information on domestic and foreign trade and on the costs of goods. The Bureau of Labor Statistics, under the Department of Labor, periodically reports on unemployment and the salaries of various personnel. The Census Bureau was empowered by the framers of the Constitution to count the number of people in the United States and to report on facts about their lives. The Departments of Education, Health and Human Services, Agriculture, and Defense use statisticians to help them plan policy to aid schoolchildren, welfare families, health-care providers, the farmer, and the guardians of strategic defense.

Statisticians also work for advertising companies, communications networks, and pollsters. These mathematicians supply information on how various segments of the country feel about consumer goods, entertainment, and political decisions. Scientific organizations use statisticians to help them analyze data in order to determine if the results of their experiments are significant or were caused by chance. Before a new food, a new drug, or a new cosmetic is sold, the manufacturer must supply the Food and Drug Administration with a detailed statistical report on the safety and effectiveness of the product.

Information scientists work with electronics firms and communications companies in the development of new ways of sending messages. The telephone company hires many communications analysts to help send spoken words, pictures, typed pages, and raw computer data instantaneously anywhere in the world. Advances in laser technology and fiber optics are being employed for new developments. Communications satellites are used by television networks and phone companies around the world. The Department of Defense, the Central Intelligence Agency, the National Aeronautics and Space Administration, the National Oceanic and Atmospheric Administration, and the Federal Aviation Administration hire information mathematicians to help them develop better communications systems.

More than half of all mathematicians and computer specialists work for private industry, businesses, and service companies. They are usually applied mathematicians who are hired to help the company make a profit and perform its duties efficiently and effectively. Mathematicians in industry usually work in teams. They often find that their real problems are in communicating their ideas to the nonmathematicians who are their managers or to the personnel who must implement their improvements.

How Can I Become a Mathematician?

A different amount of educational training is required for the various careers in mathematics. Classical and applied mathematicians usually have an advanced degree when they apply for a job. Programmers and statisticians may find employment with a bachelor's degree. College and research positions generally insist on a doctorate. Jobs for computer scientists and information specialists often require training or experience in a specialized branch of science or engineering, as well as an advanced degree in mathematics.

In high school, regardless of your planned job choice, you should take all the math and science courses available. If you want to use your mathematical skills in business, economics and other business education courses will be helpful. You will need to communicate your ideas; therefore, English coursework is essential.

Your high school math courses should include algebra II, geometry, and trigonometry. If statistics or computer science is offered, of course, take it. Biology, chemistry, and physics are required background courses if you want to use mathematics in science. Physics, especially, is the keystone to most advanced mathematics today. Courses such as astronomy, oceanography, and earth science can help you in your career but should not be taken in place of the three fundamental science courses.

A bachelor's degree in mathematics can be obtained at most colleges and universities. The math major takes courses in analytical geometry, differential equations, matrix algebra, calculus, probability, statistics, and computer programming. In addition, the student takes the English, foreign language, science, physical education, and social studies requirements of the college. Specialized coursework in physics, electronics, engineering, economics, law, and so on will give the math major training that will help in finding an interesting job.

All fields of mathematics require a knowledge of computer programming, since most complex mathematical computation is done by computer. Training in computer concepts, programming, systems analysis, and data retrieval techniques will be good preparation for any job.

Many mathematicians go immediately to graduate school after receiving their bachelor's degree. More than 400 colleges and universities have programs leading to the master's degree in mathematics, and about 150 offer the Ph.D degree. In graduate school students build upon the basic knowledge they have acquired. They specialize in a field of mathematics, in which they take advanced coursework. The Ph.D. degree requires concentrated study in a highly specialized area, as well as writing a dissertation on an original research project in mathematics. The work on a doctorate is carried out under the guidance of a team of expert mathematicians.

A classical mathematician, either applied or pure, should obtain a doctoral degree. The bachelor's degree may be adequate preparation for some jobs in private industry and government, but most employers want advanced degrees. Those bachelor's degree holders who find jobs usually assist senior mathematicians by performing computations and solving less advanced problems in applied mathematics. Others work as research or teaching assistants in colleges and universities while studying for an advanced degree.

For work in applied mathematics, training in the field in which the mathematics will be used is very important. Fields in which applied mathematics is used extensively include physics, engineering, operations research, economics, statistics, chemistry, the life sciences, medical research, and the behavioral sciences.

A bachelor's degree with a major in statistics or mathematics is the minimum educational requirement for many beginning jobs in statistics. However, some employers prefer to offer starting jobs to those with bachelor's degrees in a field such as economics or natural science with a minor in statistics. These employers, and their numbers are growing, feel that it is easier to develop the statistical skills in their new employees than to teach them the science or economic theory necessary for the job. Many jobs require an advanced degree, and university teaching generally necessitates a doctorate. Most mathematical statisticians have at least a bachelor's degree in mathematics and an advanced degree in statistics.

Beginning statisticians who have only the bachelor's degree often spend much of their time performing routine work under the supervision of an experienced statistician. Through experience, they may advance to positions of greater technical and supervisory responsibility. However, opportunities for promotion are best for those with advanced degrees.

For jobs as computer specialists employers usually want analysts with a bachelor's degree or graduate training and a background in a relevant field. For businesses, the successful applicant may have had computer and mathematics training in college, with coursework or work experience in accounting, business management, or economics. For science, technology, engineering, or more classically mathematics-related jobs, employers look for training in the physical sciences. A growing number of employers seek applicants with a degree in computer science, information science, or data processing. Regardless of college major, most employers want people who are familiar with programming languages. Courses in computer concepts, systems analysis, and data retrieval techniques offer good preparation in this field.

Prior work experience is important. Nearly half of all persons entering the computer-based occupations have transferred from other occupations.

Mathematicians need good reasoning ability, persistence, and the ability to work well with others, and they should also be able to communicate difficult ideas. They should be able to concentrate and pay close attention to details.

What Are My Chances of Getting a Job as a Mathematician or Computer Specialist?

There are about 43,000 classical mathematicians employed in this country. Only about 1,200 openings a year will develop. Persons seeking employment as classical mathematicians, either applied or theoretical, are likely to face keen competition. Many mathematicians have traditionally found jobs in colleges and universities, but these institutions are not expected to do any significant hiring throughout the next decade.

Private industry and governmental agencies will need applied mathematicians for work in operations research, numerical analysis, computer systems programming, applied physics, market research, commercial surveys, and as consultants in industrial laboratories.

There are currently about 28,000 statisticians in this country, and about 1,500 new ones will be needed each year. Private industry will require increasing numbers of statisticians for quality control in manufacturing. New government standards, economic reports, and environmental laws are compelling many concerns to release statistical data on their production.

Statisticians with a knowledge of engineering and the physical sciences will find jobs working with scientists and engineers in research and development. Business firms will rely more heavily than in the past on statisticians to forecast sales, analyze business conditions, modernize accounting procedures, and help solve management problems.

Many fields such as law, education, psychology, and history are discovering the usefulness of statistics. As the broader use of statistical methods develops, more and more colleges and universities are requiring courses in statistics for most of their students. This is producing a need for more professors of statistics and will create more jobs for statisticians.

Federal, state, and local government agencies will need statisticians for help in examining the needs of their constituencies and the effectiveness of existing programs. Welfare agencies, social security, health-care facilities, boards of education, and so on will need statisticians.

The employment of computer specialists in the 1980's is expected to grow faster than for most occupations. There should be about 9,000 openings for computer specialists each year in the next decade. There were just over 100,000 specialists in 1974, and by 1984 almost 200,000 will be employed.

Most businesses and accounting firms, all industries, all branches of government, and much scientific research and development rely on computers. The demand for computer specialists will rise as computer capabilities are increased and computers are used to solve problems in a larger variety of areas. Sophisticated accounting systems, telecommunications networks, and complex mathematical systems used in scientific research all use the new problem-solving capabilities of high-speed computers. Over the next decade, more small businesses will be installing their own computers, causing a rise in demand for specially designed computer programs geared for the problems of the small firm.

The outlook for graduates of computer-related curricula should be excellent. College graduates who have had courses in computer programming, systems analysis, and data processing with a major in business or science should find many opportunities.

Pure mathematician's jobs, however, may be difficult to obtain. College graduates with degrees in mathematics should find their background helpful for careers in other areas. Many jobs rely heavily on the application of mathematical theories and methods. Math majors are likely to find openings in statistics, actuarial work, computer programming, systems analysis, economics, engineering, and in the physical and life sciences.

New graduates may also find openings as high school mathematics teachers after completing education courses and other requirements for a state teaching certificate.

How Much Do Mathematicians and Computer Specialists Earn?

The income for people trained in mathematics is relatively high for salaried personnel. Mathematicians and statisticians who started work in 1979 earned an average yearly salary of $15,888 with a bachelor's degree, $18,024 with a master's degree, and $24,840 with a doctorate. The average salary for an experienced mathematician in 1979 was $27,500. Experienced mathematicians and statisticians earned an average of $30,000 if they were employed in private enterprise, $26,300 in universities, $22,700 in two-year colleges, $28,400 in nonprofit organizations, $30,200 in the Federal government, and $27,500 in state and local governments.

Computer specialists with a bachelor's degree started work in 1979 with an average annual salary of $16,812, and those with a master's degree started at $20,268. The average salary for experienced computer specialists in 1979 was $25,900. Experienced computer specialists in business earned $26,000; at universities, they earned $23,400; at nonprofit organizations, the average salary was $24,400; in the Federal government, it was $28,000; and state and local governments paid an average salary of $20,100.

The Federal government employs over 5,000 mathematicians, about 3,000 statisticians, and over 60,000 computer specialists. The starting salary in 1979 for those with a bachelor's degree and no experience was $11,243 or $13,925, depending on their college records. Those with a master's degree started at $17,035 or $20,611; those with Ph.D.'s started at $20,611 or $24,703. Average salaries for math specialists in the Federal government range from $24,520 to $39,742.

Jobs for mathematicians at universities are very scarce, but there are openings for statisticians and computer experts. Salaries in 1979 started at around $17,380 for people with doctorates employed at universities. The starting salary was around $14,750 at a two-year college and $16,500 at a four-year college. Salaries climb to an average of $28,770 at a university, $21,650 at a two-year college, and $24,650 at a four-year college. Some university professors earned salaries near $40,000 in 1979, but most earned far less. The average salary for school teachers in the United States in 1978–79 was $15,040.

Where Can I Obtain Training in the Mathematical Sciences?

Some of the colleges and universities that offer a major in mathematics are:

Baylor University, Waco, Texas 76703
Berea College, Berea, Kentucky 40403
Brown University, Providence, Rhode Island 02912
Carnegie-Mellon University, Pittsburgh, Pennsylvania 15213
Clemson University, Clemson, South Carolina 29631
Creighton University, Omaha, Nebraska 68131
De Paul University, Chicago, Illinois 60604
Duke University, Durham, North Carolina 27706
Eastern Michigan University, Ypsilanti, Michigan 48197
Florida A and M University, Tallahassee, Florida 32307
Fordham University, New York, N.Y. 10458
Georgia Institute of Technology, Atlanta, Georgia 30332
Illinois Institute of Technology, Chicago, Illinois 60616
Indiana University of Pennsylvania, Indiana, Pennsylvania 15701
Lehigh University, Bethlehem, Pennsylvania 18015
Lowell Technical Institute, Lowell, Massachusetts 01854
Marietta College, Marietta, Ohio 45750
Massachusetts Institute of Technology, Cambridge, Massachusetts 02139
Miami University, Oxford, Ohio 45056
Michigan Technical University, Houghton, Michigan 49931
Mississippi State University, State College, Mississippi 39762
Mount Holyoke College, South Hadley, Massachusetts 01075
New York University, New York, N.Y. 10003
Northern Arizona University, Flagstaff, Arizona 86001
Oberlin College, Oberlin, Ohio 44074
University of Oregon, Eugene, Oregon 97403
Pan American University, Edinburg, Texas 78539
Providence College, Providence, Rhode Island 02918
Purdue University, West Lafayette, Indiana 47907
University of Rochester, Rochester, New York 14627
Rutgers University, New Brunswick, New Jersey 08903
Seton Hall University, South Orange, New Jersey 07079
Southern Methodist University, Dallas, Texas 75275
St. Bonaventure University, St. Bonaventure, New York 14778
St. John Fisher College, Rochester, New York 14618
Temple University, Philadelphia, Pennsylvania 19122
Tufts University, Medford, Massachusetts 02155
U.S. Naval Academy, Annapolis, Maryland 21402
Utica College, Utica, New York 13502
Virginia Polytechnic Institute, Blacksburg, Virginia 24601
Washington University, St. Louis, Missouri 63130
West Virginia Institute of Technology, Montgomery, West Virginia 25136

College of William and Mary, Williamsburg, Virginia 23185
Worcester State College, Worcester, Massachusetts 01602
Yale University, New Haven, Connecticut 06520

Some of the colleges and universities that offer a major in computer science are:

American University, Washington, D.C. 20016
University of Arkansas, Fayetteville, Arkansas 72701
Auburn College, Auburn, New York 13021
Bates College, Lewiston, Maine 04240
Boston College, Chestnut Hill, Massachusetts 02167
Bowling Green State University, Bowling Green, Ohio 43403
Bradley University, Peoria, Illinois 61606
Brown University, Providence, Rhode Island 02912
Bucknell University, Lewisburg, Pennsylvania 17837
Clarkson College of Technology, Potsdam, New York 13676
Dartmouth College, Hanover, New Hampshire 03755
Denison University, Granville, Ohio 43023
University of Detroit, Detroit, Michigan 48221
Dowling College, Oakdale, New York 11769
Drexel Institute of Technology, Philadelphia, Pennsylvania 19104
Elmira College, Elmira, New York 14901
Fordham University, New York, N.Y. 10458
Goucher College, Towson, Maryland 21204
Harper College, Palatine, Illinois 60067
Harvard University, Cambridge, Massachusetts 02138
Haverford College, Haverford, Pennsylvania 19041
University of Houston, Houston, Texas 77004
University of Idaho, Moscow, Idaho 83843
University of Iowa, Iowa City, Iowa 52242
University of Kansas, Lawrence, Kansas 66045
Lamar University, Beaumont, Texas 77710
Long Island University, New York, N.Y. 11201
Louisiana Polytechnic Institute, Ruston, Louisiana 71270
Loyola College, Baltimore, Maryland 21210
University of Maryland, College Park, Maryland 20742
Massachusetts Institute of Technology, Cambridge, Massachusetts 02139
Miami University, Oxford, Ohio 45056
University of Michigan, Ann Arbor, Michigan 48104
Middlebury College, Middlebury, Vermont 05753
Montana State University, Bozeman, Montana 59715
Morehouse College, Atlanta, Georgia 30314
Mount Holyoke College, South Hadley, Massachusetts 01075
University of Nebraska, Lincoln, Nebraska 68508
New Hampshire College, Manchester, New Hampshire 03104
University of New Mexico, Albuquerque, New Mexico 87131
New York University, New York, N.Y. 10003

North Carolina State University, Raleigh, North Carolina 27607
Northeastern Illinois University, Chicago, Illinois 60625
Norwich University, Northfield, Vermont 05663
Notre Dame College, Cleveland, Ohio 44121
Ohio State University, Columbus, Ohio 43212
Ohio University, Athens, Ohio 45701
Pace University, New York, N.Y. 10038, and Pleasantville, New York 10570
University of Pennsylvania, Philadelphia, Pennsylvania 19104
Pennsylvania State University, University Park, Pennsylvania 16802
University of Pittsburgh, Pittsburgh, Pennsylvania 15213
University of Portland, Portland, Oregon 97203
Pratt Institute, New York, N.Y. 11205
Purdue University (Lafayette, Calumet, and North Central), West Lafayette, Indiana 47907; Hammond, Indiana 46323; and Westville, Indiana 46391
Rider College, Trenton, New Jersey 08602
University of Rochester, Rochester, New York 14627
Rochester Institute of Technology, Rochester, New York 14623
Rutgers University, New Brunswick, New Jersey 08903
Southern Illinois University, Edwardsville, Illinois 62025
St. Peter's College, Jersey City, New Jersey 07307
State University of New York, Alfred, Stony Brook, Cobleskill and Morrisville, New York
Stevens Institute of Technology, Hoboken, New Jersey 07030
Swarthmore College, Swarthmore, Pennsylvania 19081
University of Toledo, Toledo, Ohio 43614
Union College, Lincoln, Nebraska 68506
Valparaiso Institute of Technology, Valparaiso, Indiana 46383
Virginia Commonwealth University, Richmond, Virginia 23284
Wayne State University, Detroit, Michigan 48202
Wentworth Institute, Boston, Massachusetts 02115
Wesleyan University, Middletown, Connecticut 06457
West Coast University, Los Angeles, California 90020
West Liberty State College, West Liberty, West Virginia 26074
West Virginia University, Morgantown, West Virginia 26506
Western Michigan University, Kalamazoo, Michigan 49001
Westminster College, Fulton, Missouri 65251
Williams College, Williamstown, Massachusetts 01267
Worcester Polytechnic Institute, Worcester, Massachusetts 01520

Where Can I Obtain More Information About the Mathematical Sciences?

For information on careers in mathematics write to:

American Mathematical Society
Box 6248
Providence, RI 02904

Mathematical Association of America
1225 Connecticut Avenue N.W.
Washington, DC 20036

Institute of Mathematical Statistics
Department of Statistics
California State College at Hayward
Hayward, CA 94542

Society for Industrial and Applied Mathematics
33 South 17th Street
Philadelphia, PA 19103

For information on careers in the computer sciences write to:

American Federation of Information Processing Societies
210 Summit Avenue
Montvale, NJ 07645

Data Processing Management Association
505 Busse Highway
Park Ridge, IL 60068

For Federal job information write to:

Interagency Board of U.S. Civil Service Examiners
1900 E Street N.W.
Washington, DC 20415

For more detailed information, you may want to read:

Your Future in the Electronic Computer Field by D. L. Bibby. Richards
   Rosen Press, Inc.
Your Future in Computer Programming by S. Davis. Richards Rosen Press,
   Inc.